Greed

Pride

Michael Eric Dyson

Envy

Joseph Epstein

Anger

Robert A. F. Thurman

Sloth

Wendy Wasserstein

Greed

Phyllis A. Tickle

Gluttony

Francine Prose

Lust

Simon Blackburn

For over a decade, The New York Public Library and Oxford University Press have annually invited a prominent figure in the arts and letters to give a series of lectures on a topic of his or her choice. Subsequently these lectures become the basis of a book jointly published by the Library and the Press. For 2002 and 2003 the two institutions asked seven noted writers, scholars, and critics to offer a "meditation on temptation" on one of the seven deadly sins. *Greed* by Phyllis A. Tickle is the fourth book from this lecture series.

Previous books from The New York Public Library/Oxford University Press Lectures are:

Also by Phyllis A. Tickle

Greed

The Seven Deadly Sins

Phyllis A. Tickle

The New York Public Library

OXFORD
UNIVERSITY PRESS

OXFORD

UNIVERSITY PRESS

Oxford University Press, Inc., publishes works that
further Oxford University's objective of excellence
in research, scholarship, and education.

Oxford   New York
Auckland   Cape Town   Dar es Salaam   Hong Kong   Karachi
Kuala Lumpur   Madrid   Melbourne   Mexico City   Nairobi
New Delhi   Shanghai   Taipei   Toronto

With offices in
Argentina   Austria   Brazil   Chile   Czech Republic   France   Greece
Guatemala   Hungary   Italy   Japan   Poland   Portugal   Singapore
South Korea   Switzerland   Thailand   Turkey   Ukraine   Vietnam

First published by Oxford University Press, Inc., 2004
198 Madison Avenue, New York, NY 10016
www.oup.com

First issued as an Oxford University Press paperback, 2006
ISBN-13: 978-0-19-531206-5

Oxford is a registered trademark of Oxford University Press

The Library of Congress has cataloged the hardcover edition as follows:
Tickle, Phyllis A.
Greed : the seven deadly sins / Phyllis A. Tickle.
p. cm.
Includes bibliographical references and index.

1. Avarice—Religious aspects—Christianity.
I. Title. II. Series.
BV4627.A8T53 2004
179'.8—dc21   2003048686 Rev.

9 8 7 6 5 4 3

Printed in the United States of America
on acid-free paper

for Kate, D.C. and Brian, Wade, and Ben,
all newly come into this life.

May theirs be a time of holy imagination.

Mario Donizetti, *Avarice*, 1996, encaustic pastel.

Contents

Editor's Note

This volume is part of a lecture and book series on the Seven Deadly Sins cosponsored by The New York Public Library and Oxford University Press. Our purpose was to invite scholars and writers to chart the ways we have approached and understood evil, one deadly sin at a time. Through both historical and contemporary explorations, each writer finds the conceptual and practical challenges that a deadly sin poses to spirituality, ethics, and everyday life.

The notion of the Seven Deadly Sins did not originate in the Bible. Sources identify early lists of transgressions classified in the 4th century by Evagrius of Pontus and then by John of Cassius. In the 6th century, Gregory the Great formulated the traditional seven. The sins were ranked by increasing severity, and judged to be the greatest offenses to the soul and the root of all other sins. As certain sins were subsumed into others and similar terms were used interchangeably according to theological review, the list evolved to include the seven as we know them: Pride, Greed, Lust, Envy, Gluttony, Anger, and Sloth. To counter these violations, Christian theologians classified the Seven Heavenly Virtues—the cardinal: Prudence, Temperance, Justice, Fortitude, and the theological: Faith, Hope, and Charity. The sins inspired medieval and Renaissance writers including Chaucer, Dante, and Spenser, who personified the seven in rich and memorable characters. Depictions grew to include associated colors, animals, and punishments in hell for the deadly offenses. Through history, the famous list has emerged in theological and philosophical tracts, psychology, politics, social criticism, popular culture, and art and literature. Whether the deadly seven to you represent the most common human foibles or more serious spiritual shortcomings, they stir the imagination and evoke the inevitable question—what is *your* deadly sin?

Our contemporary fascination with these age-old sins, our struggle against or celebration of them, reveals as much about our continued desire to define human nature as it does about our divine aspirations. I hope that this book and its companions invite the reader to indulge in a similar reflection on vice, virtue, the spiritual, and the human.

Elda Rotor

Greed

Being a
Bit of Context

A religion editor for a trade journal—which is what I am and of whom, believe me, there are not many—functions as a student of religion commercially applied. From that perspective, religion is most accurately seen as a rope or cable of meaning that stretches through human history and has anchored, in one form or another, every culture or subculture of human society from its beginning. Like any good and anchoring cable, this one too is composed of strands. In religion's case, the strands are three in number: spirituality, corporeality, and morality. As components in a larger whole, the three are held together by the porous, inner sleeve of a common or shared imagination and then protected by an outer casing or skin that we most commonly refer to as story.

Historically, the rope of meaning—of religion—will hold a society or a people in place for decades, sometimes even centuries, before some cultural shift or event causes a break or unraveling in the story and a pocking of the imagination. When that rupture of the protective casing and the insulating sleeve occurs, inevitably the three working strands, which are always discrete even as they are intertwined, are exposed to view. Once that has happened, the effected culture must begin all over again the business of lifting each strand separately up through the sleeve and out of the cable, fingering and inspecting it to satisfaction, and then returning it to a place in the braid of the cable, though that new positioning is never quite identical to its prior one. Eventually, once a culture is done with investigating all three strands and has replaced them, the mesh sleeve is smoothed back around their union, and the rip in the story is knitted back together again. The cable is restored, good as new, to its rightful duties for a while longer.

Every undergraduate can name with ease times when, the casing having been stripped back and its lining pitted, our forefathers have had to interpret, or mend, the story and weave the inner sleeve in order to make the cable hold again. The Babylonian Captivity was certainly such a time for Judaism, as was the axial era for several faiths. More pivotal for most Euro-Americans, of course, the Renaissance, the Reformation, and the Enlightenment each challenged especially the Judeo-Christian story and demanded that Western culture consider the strands of the rope once more.

For contemporary readers, however, the peeling away of religion's story to expose religion's constituent parts is not just a matter of remembered or academically acquired history. It is also very much one of lived experience—recently and presently lived experience. During the twentieth century and especially during its latter half, the West and most dramatically, America, passed through—indeed, is still passing through the end of—a time as rupturing, configuring, and informing for religion as was, for instance, either the axial era or the Reformation.[1]

From Albert Schweitzer's first agonized cry of protest in 1906 that the Christ of history just might not be the Jesus of first century Nazareth, to the descent of the Spirit upon the congregations gathering on Azusa Street in Los Angeles that same year;

——from the founding and rampant success of Alcoholics Anonymous in 1935 with its emphasis on self- or group-help and its reverencing of a higher, but not doctrinally specific power, to the archeology and caprices of fortune that would give us Nag Hammadi and Qumran with their variant texts of, and variant commentary upon, our accepted story;

————from the Second World War with its Holocaust horrors that sent thousands of Europe's brightest and most able Jews to live in the United States as welcome agents of victory and thereafter as appreciated and accepted fellow-citizens, to the change in 1965 of immigration laws that for the first time in decades allowed people of Asian descent (people, we must note, who for centuries had lived in the subjective and spiritual world as naturally as they had lived in the objective one) to come among us less-lately-come Americans, bringing with them their spiritual riches;

————from the discovery of antibiotics and the unprecedented advances in medicine's ability to miraculously heal, to the urbanization and mobility that ruptured the nuclear family;

————from the magnificent silence of the Big Bang and an explored outer space, to the postulates of chaos physics;

————from the rise of radio and inexpensive publishing to the establishment of the internet that enfranchised popular culture and spawned the democratization of information.

From these and at least two dozen more equally dynamic shifts and pivotal points in Western culture have come the changed circumstances and perceptions that have unraveled and slipped back both the cable's casing and its lining, leaving twentieth-century Western culture to finger its way through the mesh and explore as it may the strands of meaning that had for decades lain strong, but dormant, there.[2]

As a people of many faiths and cultures but one polity, Americans dealt first, during the last century, with spirituality. As AA taught adult Americans more about the spiritual world and as Buddhism and science showed us more and more about how to map and traverse it, we began to gain a kind of comfort and ease or, if you will, a surcease through familiarity. In time the naivete of that position matured, and we began to stuff spirituality back into its sustaining and rightful place in the cable. As a result, it is now more appreciated among us than it was a century ago, but it is also considerably less voguish than it was, for instance, three decades ago.

The second strand, which we lifted out and began to inspect in the last century, was corporeality, a bulky term that refers to all the overt and institutionalized evidences of religion—its real estate, clergy, administrative and professional hierarchies, institutions of learning and healing, canons, requirements of membership, legal status, budgets, etc. The last forty-odd years, from Vatican II to today's evening news, have been a veritable carnival of medieval proportions in ecclesial adjustments and adjustments, as most North Americans indeed know.

Ecumenism and shared communion, revised hymnals and written prayer books, world and national and multinational councils, the ordination of women and lately of homosexuals, integration and apology, the interface of church and state and the proper definitions thereof, the use of heavy endowments as political tools, the use of ecclesial stature in international affairs, the usurping of authority and power by laity, the rise of Pentecostalism—this list too goes almost endlessly on, each member part of it telling the story of a foment that is close to completing, in fact probably has completed, the work of the Reformation and brought to its natural end an era of 500 years of rampant divisiveness and sectarianism. We are not done with our fingering of corporeality, of course; but as with spirituality, we are already beginning to stuff wisps and fibers of it back into place.

That leaves us with morality, the strand of religion that we most dread and that our times are just beginning to lift out for intense inspection. Indeed, we have so lately come to attending the strand of morality that in all probability we have not even shaped the subset of particulars that will become the questions of our next quarter century.

Morality, because it effects and governs conduct, both private and corporate, is the wiriest part of religion's cable and the one most susceptible to secularization. Thus, when morality adulterates with schemes of action and values other than religion, and especially when it slips its encasement in story and inter- twines itself with them, it becomes something one may more accurately call a code of conduct, or a system of values, rather than of meaning; or to use the twentieth century's term that first heralded this shift in our times, it becomes an exercise in "situational ethics." That is to say that while all of these things may indeed be matters of morality, they are to the degree of their adulteration more political, philosophical, even utilitarian, to borrow another old term, tools than they are religion.

Vietnam and hypnotic Americanism, like divorce, abortion, and gender, may have been the opening battle cries of our new engagement with morality as a strand of religion, but they were as nothing compared to the questions that lie ahead. In particular, as science, medicine, theology, and philosophy probe ever more skillfully into the nature of human mentation and subjective and/or spiritual structure, including into the evolution of human consciousness, this culture will be faced with issues of human responsibility and training and social management, even of human manipulation, for which no prior intellectual guidelines exist and for which there is not yet a fully realized shared imagination.

Most Americans realize that this tsunami is visible on the horizon, whether we think about it every day with intention or not; and most of us have held the questions attendant to it consciously, if *sotto voce*, in our heads for at least two decades. We have acknowledged their impending arrival enough even to begin some of the initial work that will be required for our survival as a civilization. We have come to imagine and sometimes admit, albeit tentatively, that even public morality must of necessity have its roots in the private morality of its citizens. We have begun once more to imagine that private morality is a religious issue not only in theocratic states like ancient Israel or much of contemporary Islam or pre-Reformation Europe but also for the majority in democratic America. Here, while we may not agree with one another religiously, we do believe, at a ratio of nine to one, in adherence to some religious system. We also seem to agree that if religion is not in and of itself the basis for morality, it is nonetheless the litmus test for what morality can and cannot include.

This train of thought, however subtle in its tracking, has traveled slowly, but more directly than circuitously, to a growing, popular consideration of morality itself, to a consideration not so much of what constitutes it, as to what causes violations of it. At a popular level, the most arresting evidence of this progression is the return of sin to the cultural conversation: When, for instance, one sees pop music groups named "Sin" or some play on words including it, when one sees phenomenally popular games named "Sin," when one sees website after website focusing on sin, even when one sees smart and successful books like Lyall Watson's *Dark Nature: A Natural History of Evil*[3] or John Portmann's recent *In Defense of Sin*,[4] which are in content exactly what their titles suggest.

When one sees these things and more, then the presence of an increasing American preoccupation with sin as a concept is as confirmed as it ever can be, short of some longitudinal study that, so far as I know, never has been attempted nor ever could be logistically feasible. I must observe, however, though just as an aside, that the decision by Oxford University Press and the New York Public Library to make the Seven Deadly Sins the subjects in 2002 and 2003 for their jointly sponsored series of lectures likewise offers its own kind of witness to an increasing absorption with questions of evil.[5] I would also mention, primarily because it is obvious and because I want to return to it briefly elsewhere, that a preoccupation with sin during the decades surrounding an era of apocalyptic anxiety is both predictable and historically consistent, which does not mean to suggest that our present and recent fixation upon it is any less valid or real.

However we may document the increasing presence of sin in our awareness, though, the fact is that any discussion of sin leads, within minutes, if not seconds, to a discussion of the reasons for it, the thinking behind it, the nature of its mechanisms, even its possible uses. In that line of business, my own tradition of Christianity has led the way, sometimes to levels of fascination and intricacy that can only be called fatuous, if not downright silly.

All of that is to say that while the world's faiths may be persuaded of the spiritual ramifications of vice's presence in human life, they nonetheless differ to some greater or lesser degree not only in how they envision vice, but also in the relative emphasis they place on its role in the spirit's and/or soul's progress toward goodness. The most marked differences, understandably, are between the so-called Eastern religions and those that over the last several millennia have managed to thrive in Mideastern and Western culture. Thus the Abrahamic faiths of the desert have produced a whole theology and cosmology of evil, whereas the traditions of less arid and more populace Asia have tended to show a far greater interest in developing a philosophy or theology of virtue. Humility, charity, and veracity are emphasized within the Asian faiths, where they are taught as tools necessary to ward off or overcome sins, which are regarded as "obstacles," so to speak, to the exercise of virtue. The Buddha, for instance, identified greed, hatred, and delusion as impediments to right living, naming them as "three poisons" rather than as created agencies. This latter conceptualization of agency belongs more to the sons of Abraham. Even more exclusively, what Henry Fairlie calls "the idea of sin as a construct" belongs to Christianity; for no other of the world's religions has ever so completely embodied or embroidered sin as has the Christian one.[6]

Whether one be a Christian or an adherent of another of the Abrahamic faiths or even whether one be a theist or nontheist or atheist, however, one still must acknowledge the presence of that which appears to be—has indeed always been held to be—universally human. We must confess, each of us, that the human animal seems to come into the experience of time constructed and equipped not only with body parts and consciousness, but also with inescapable companions of the interior that historically we have often referred to as our demons. While that term may be etymologically accurate, it is no longer popularly so; for "demon," from the time when Jewish and Christian writers first usurped it until very recently, has incontestably connoted evil or destructiveness in popular usage, whereas the truth is that these taunting companions of ours can prod us into well-being as well as destruction.[7] Indeed without them we will die just as because of them we are condemned to die. They are usually listed as being seven in number,[8] these invisible companions of ours, and the conundrum they posit is the second death from which the Christian seeks salvation just as surely as they are the torment from which the Buddhist seeks release in his or her search for nothingness through the subjugation of desire.

Despite all the eons of human struggle, however, and under the rubrics of any faith, the seven still reenter our being with the birth of every child; and with every new child, we, as coinhabitants of time, and they, as emerging agencies of time, must engage all over again the intricacy of the seven and their chameleon-like ability to change from virtue to vice and back again in the wink of an eye. Without the fascinating seven, we human beings would never rest or eat or procreate or build or aspire. We would also, however, never sedate ourselves with drugs or gorge or suffer an epidemic of AIDS; nor, for that matter, would we murder, steal, or lie. Without them, we would not, in other words, be human; for we are instruments of a tension held in place by, and ticking in place only because of, the arc or slide of the pendulum between the virtues of courage, faith, fortitude, love, hope, prudence, and justice and their corresponding alter egos of pride, envy, anger, lust, sloth, gluttony, and greed.

Christianity, the predominant religious system in the West, calls those seven vices the seven deadly sins and has since its beginnings in Galilee.[9] The interchangeability of vice with sin may not be exclusively a Christian foible, but it is most certainly an inelegant one for the rest of the world's faith communions in that it blurs the line between what is universal in humanity's construction and the exercise of an act that does not, in and of itself, have to be.[10] But whether a religious system conflates or separates vice and sin, the truth remains that every system from Hinduism to Christianity has agreed over the centuries that of our seven demons, greed is the mistress. Hinduism in particular leaves little question about the primacy of greed in the scheme of things. *The Mahabharata*, Santi Parva, Section CLVIII teaches thus:

> Yudhisthira said: I desire, O bull of Bharata's race, to hear in detail the source from which sin proceeds and the foundation on which it rests.
>
> Bhishma said: Hear, O King, what the foundation is of sin. Covetousness alone is a great destroyer of merit and goodness. From covetousness proceeds sin. It is from this source that sin and irreligiousness flow, together with great misery. This covetousness is the spring also of all the cunning and hypocrisy in the world. It is covetousness that makes men commit sin . . . it is from covetousness that loss of judgment, deception, pride, arrogance, and malice, as also vindictiveness, loss of prosperity, loss of virtue, anxiety, and infamy spring. Miserliness, cupidity, desire for every kind of improper act, pride of birth, pride of learning, pride of beauty, pride of wealth, pitilessness for all creatures, malevolence towards all, mistrust in respect of all, insincerity towards all, appropriation of other people's wealth . . . all these proceed from covetousness.

Bhishma and Hinduism are hardly alone among the world's religions in this understanding of greed, however. Buddhism, in essence, rests on a practiced abhorrence for the desires and ways of desiring that we gather under any one of several names: "greed," "covetousness," "avarice," "cupidity." Thus the *Visuddhimagga* (XII) counsels both the Buddhist and the non-Buddhist by explicit instruction:

> Greed is the real dirt, not dust;
> Greed is the term for real dirt.
> The wise have shaken off this dirt,
> And in the dirt-free man's religion, live.

The *Tao Teh Ching* tells us that "There is no greater calamity than indulging in greed"; and The *Guru Granth Sahib* or *Adi Granth*, the holy book which is both the supreme spiritual authority as well as the living head of the Sikh religion, delivers the same news as a telling question: "Where there is greed, what love can there be?"

In Judaism, long before Sinai and the giving to Moses of the Law, there was Noah and the seven laws or *mishpathim* that are presented, one by one, incident by incident, in the first eleven chapters of the book of Genesis. Known as The Seven Laws of Noah, they were the governing principles of Judaism before Sinai and, by their early coming, sketched in the first parameters of Jewish moral and religious thought. The Seven Laws of Noah are couched, as nine of the Ten Commandments are later, in terms of sins that must not be committed. In order of their biblical occurrence, the first *mishpat* or sin is blasphemy; the second is idolatry; the third, theft; the fourth, murder; the fifth, illicit sex; the sixth, false witness or duplicity in adjudication; and the last, the eating of flesh torn from a living beast. Of these, many rabbis came in time to teach that theft was the greatest, because all the others depend from it. To commit adultery is to steal another's partner. To blaspheme is to steal the name of G-d for human purposes. To commit murder is to steal another's life, etc., and theft comes out of greed or covetousness.[11]

Thus it is that Judaism exposes for us greed's second, and beyond current and historical ubiquity, its most obvious characteristic, prolixity, commencing with the plethora of names assigned it over the centuries. Ever true to its own acquisitive nature, greed has functioned under a multiplicity of aliases ranging from "acquisitiveness" itself to "covetousness," "avidity," "cupidity," "avarice," and on to some of its more particularized metonyms like "miserliness" or, of course, "simony," the most recently coined of the lot (ca. 1175 C.E.) and a label for what is probably greed's most egregious permutation.[12]

Indeed, greed, by any name, is the mother and matrix, root and consort of all the other sins; and it is to this matriarch of a deadly clan that we now turn our attention.

Being a Study of Less Than Three Parts

This essay on greed that, like the sin it treats, is only one in a suite of seven, is an expansion with annotations of a lecture first delivered at the New York Public Library in October, 2002, where it served as one paper in a series of lectures sponsored jointly each year by the library and Oxford University Press. The choice of "The Seven Deadly Sins" as the topic for 2002's lecture series had been made some two years earlier in late 2000. I mention this here because no one I know, least of all me, would have been intrepid enough in 2002 to agree willingly to deliver a public lecture on the subject of greed in the heart of Manhattan. Such a proposition, however, had seemed imminently reasonable and even diverting to me in the more halcyon days of 2000 before Chairman Greenspan made his diagnosis of our national illness as being that of "infectious greed."[13] There have, in other words, been many times over the months of working first on the lecture and then on the present essay when I positively yearned for a more socially agreeable sin like lust or a more socially acceptable one like plain, old, all-American gluttony. But the die had been cast and the Rubicon crossed. Greed it was and greed it was destined to remain.

The truth is that, in addition to my expanding sense of trepidation about the whole matter, especially after the autumn of 2001 as scandal after scandal was followed by exposé after exposé, I also found myself becoming sated with greed, even wearied, for lack of a better word—wearied with it almost into nonchalance, in fact. My suspicion is that a lot of adult Americans were, actually. Nonchalance, where greed is concerned, however, is a fool's attitude. Thus, I came in time to believe that as a corrective—though hopefully pleasant—change of pace, I might most effectively clear my head and interrupt my own tedium as well as that of my hearers and readers, if I were to look at greed from the long view of the history of the common era rather than from the immediacy of 2002's headlines and evening newscasts. This seemed to me to be especially likely if I were to do my looking imagistically rather than didactically.

There was an additional and very practical impetus toward this choice as well, namely that sin in any of its forms is so vaporous and diffuse that ultimately it can be addressed only as an abstraction or as a presence. As an abstraction, sin tends fairly quickly to become more a theory than an integer; yet as a presence, it almost always requires an image to serve as its vehicle if it is to be entered into human conversation. Both approaches, as we shall see, have certainly been followed over the last 2,000 years; but always the images have been, and remain, not only more fun than the theories to think about but also, in the end, infinitely more informing as well. This latter observation, by the way, is perhaps of even more pertinence for the readers of an essay than for those who engage its content only as hearers of its thesis in lecture form. In addition to the luxury of being able to pace one's intake of material to meet one's own needs and pleasure, the reader has the singular advantage of end notes and authorial asides. Having become over the years a great admirer of the conversational aside, I have indulged myself here, inserting them with what can only be called abandon. I have succumbed to this penchant of mine in the belief that asides not only enrich and spice the content, but that they also give the presentation of it a bit of the human engagement that traditionally has been the lecture's most obvious advantage. So thus to those readers of like mind, my greetings; but with equal goodwill, to those who find meanderings tediously off-target, my apologies.

Meanwhile, in my desire to consider sin imagistically, whether with or without sidebars and notes, there is of course at least one rather considerable danger: art is always more persuasive than dogma under any set of circumstances, but of course it is also slyer in its conquest of our thinking. To do what I have set out to do, in other words, assumes on my part a prior interpretation of the history of the last 2,000 years; and since this is a monologue and not a dialogue per se, I need to lay out openly my own take on these ages in the name of critical fairness.

Ten years as a religion editor for a trade journal have taught me many things, some of them undoubtedly irrelevant, if not outright suspect; but it has convicted me as well of many other, worthier concepts, one of them pertinent here. The common era can be divided and subdivided, as we all know, into at least a dozen periods or segments—the early Middle Ages from the late ones, Classicism from Enlightenment, etc. But above all that slicing and dicing, there are three—or actually two and a fraction—overarching sets of sensibilities that order the various periods. The first 1,500 years, more or less (there being no clean moment of division), are a whole; and the second 400 plus are another whole. The fraction is now, which by the way, is what I'm convicted of.

The first of these eras traditionally we have named as that of the religious imagination, and the second as the era of the secular imagination. Those labels of religious and secular, however, while accurate enough to have lasted a long while, are also, in my opinion, just incorrect enough to be obscuring. We would be better served, I believe, by regarding the first fifteen hundred years as the centuries of the physical imagination, and the latter four hundred plus as the time of the intellectual imagination. The fraction, as you may have guessed, I believe is/will be that of the spiritual imagination, if in all this we understand imagination to reference the informing sensibility or seat of the attention during any given period of time. In order to observe greed as it makes its way to us over the common era, then, I want to take one or two images from each grand division and one or two from the segue between them, seeing what greed can tell us about us, as well as about herself, in this grand progression.

Paul, being the first Christian, is obviously the segue into the common era as well as the author of Christianity's first imaging of greed. *Radix omnium malorum avaritia,* wrote St. Paul to the early Church.[14] We translate that rather badly as "The love of money is the root of all evil"; but Paul certainly had an authority other than his own to support the assessment he made, however translated. Antecedent to the apostle's earliest formalizations of doctrine, the Christian Gospels treat the issues of wealth, especially of individual wealth, quite frequently. Passage after passage admonishes those who would follow the Way that they must sell all they have and disperse the money to the poor, thereby buying for themselves a place in the Kingdom of God. These are not easy instructions to follow, but for at least two decades before Paul, they became—and have remained for us as—the Christian ideal.

It is equally true that as the cornerstone and foundation of monasticism, the path of intentional poverty lived with *caritas*, while it may be the ordained and holy way, is nonetheless blocked for most believers by other vocations. Whether the Christian believer assigns responsibility for his or her failure in this regard to necessity, to other and honorable responsibilities, to a more palatable exegesis, or to outright personal failure, he or she is always aware of being, thanks to greed, just a little bit less than truly Christian in the fullest—that usually should be understood as Saint Francis of Assisi defined—sense of things. The truth in this is that we in our Christianized culture are very conflicted about Greed, and she absolutely loves us for it, which is another thing that any treatise on her must acknowledge. For either a sin or a virus, conflict in one's intended host is a compromising and very desirable thing, a fact that Greed appreciates far more astutely than we ever will.[15]

Translated in any fashion, however, the metaphorical root of Paul's *radix omnium malorum avaritia* flourished as an image, primarily visually and primarily in church murals and frescos, all over Europe until about the fifteenth century.[16] It is not the use of his image as such that interests us most, however. Rather, it is Paul's Latin sentence itself. Even as the early church accepted the apostle's warning about *avaritia* as the root of all evils, the evolving church came to employ his words with a sense of humor as well as of proper theological sobriety. Especially, in the fourth and fifth centuries, as the corruption of a failing empire became more and more oppressive, the devout took to writing Paul's doctrine stacked as an acrostic, making of it a kind of political cartoon as well as a cautionary dictum:

*R*adix (the root)
*O*mnium (of all)
*M*alorum (evils)
*A*varitia (avarice).

It is the kind of graphic punning and cartooning that has characterized greed more than any other of the sins in the common era, primarily because greed is the most social and by extension the most political of the sins. In addition, because greed is the most ubiquitous of the sins, more of us have a great need to deflect public attention off ourselves and onto others rather quickly, lest somebody suspect us of being infected as well. What better way to distract diagnostic attention, in other words, than with good graffiti?[17]

Leaving Paul's visual usages behind, however, the image that I want to deal with from the hegemony of the physical imagination comes some 350 years later from a Briton named Aurelius Clemens Prudentius and his *Psychomachia*. Translated, that title means "Soul Battle" or "Battle for the Soul." An epic-length allegory, the poem was enormously popular from the time Prudentius wrote it in ca. 405 C.E. until the fifteenth century when it dropped from the cultural canon with the demise of its era.

In addition to his *radix/roma* idea, Paul had, from the beginning, proposed that the holy life for Christians was one of holy warfare. The faithful were to take up the weapons of faith, truth, righteousness, the gospel of peace, salvation, and the word of the Spirit in order to quench all the flaming arrows of the evil one in their struggle against the principalities and cosmic powers of what Paul called "this present darkness." All Prudentius did, in effect, was to take this conceit of Paul's and, quite literally, flesh it out. The truth of the matter, of course, is that Prudentius had a considerable amount of help as well as good company in making this leap. Indeed, Paul's conceit of the believer as armed combatant and of this world as an arena of gladiatorial-like contest rather quickly became the esthetic foundation and a first principle of Western art, thought, and theology for the first 1,500 years of Christendom.

For example, Tertullian, a late second-century African theologian (ca. 160–225 C.E.), was one of the early Church's most influential writers, in no small part because he was an adult convert from paganism to Christianity. His work, to say the very least about it, reflects all the customary passion and certitude of the adult convert; and as often as not, Tertullian would evangelize and persuade as a moralist by functioning as a social commentator upon the ills of the paganism from which he had himself come. His most celebrated work in this genre is *De spectaculis.* As its title would suggest, the treatise is one long homily of sorts against all the "spectacles" of Rome—its games, circuses, plays, sports contests, etc.

It is in *De Spectaculis* that Tertullian argues—earnestly and cogently—that for Christians the more appropriate contests or *spectacula* are those between the virtues and the vices, between, for example, chastity and unchastity or faithfulness and perfidy.[18] In so doing and presumably with no deliberate intention in that direction, Tertullian breathed the breath of very long life into Paul's metaphor of spiritual warfare by rendering it in terms of all the color, excitement, and naughty imagery of the hedonistic games he himself so much opposed. Out of that chance juxtaposing of dictum with imagery was to come the fecund tradition to which we must now turn our attention.

The *Psychomachia* is the story of seven extreme battles, one for each deadly sin, in which each of the sins is personified as a human being and in each of which more ordinary human beings serve as both the minions and the prizes of each sin's engagements, which most assuredly are all exercises in bloody carnage. It is, in point of fact, with Prudentius and his use of graphic detail in presenting the sins in human guise that the literary genre of personification allegory is born into Western literature;[19] and personification allegory was to prove itself a fertile vehicle for its era, giving us most famously, of course, from today's point of view, Spenser's parade of the sins in the *Faerie Queene*;[20] and from an earlier point of view the "Moralities" or Morality plays that were Prudentius's theatrical progeny and flourished in the fifteenth and early sixteenth centuries.[21]

But what interests us here is Prudentius and his personification of Greed and her battles.[22] As the story begins, Luxury actually precedes Greed or *avaritia* onto the field of battle where she is defeated by Sobriety.[23] In this initial melee, Lust flees, dropping her bow and poisoned darts; Vanity is stripped naked and her robes dragged off; Allurement's garlands are shredded; Strife's gold ornaments and jewels are scattered; Pleasure flees barefoot through the thorns; and the battlefield itself is littered with all the garments, appointments, abandoned weapons, and apparel that such a violent contest would occasion.[24]

It is at this point that Greed herself enters the decimated field and, predictably enough, sets out to harvest the scene of battle and its dead for all their trinkets. As she does so, she holds in her left hand a bag that she has hastily cobbled together out of her own robes while with what Prudentius calls the "rake-like" fingers on her right hand, she shifts through the debris of war. Greed is accompanied in this endeavor by Care, Hunger, Fear, Anxiety, Perjury, Dread, Fraud, Fabrication, Sleeplessness, and Sordidness.[25] As this unholy company does its work of salvage, it is joined by all the crimes that are, as Prudentius says and I quote him, "the brood of their mother Greed's black milk." Murder, pillage, scavenging of the dead, civil war, pride of possession . . . the list goes on and on . . . until the poet tells us that "like ravenous wolves, her young prowl across the field."[26]

"Neque est uiolentius ullum/terrarum Vitium" (Of all the vices there is none more frightening) we are told, for (Greed wraps the lives of men in calamities that they only escape when they are thrown to Hell's fire) *"quod tantis cladibus, aeuum/mundani inuoluat populi damnetque gehennae."*[27, 28]

As if to prove her utter depravity, Greed next decides to try her hand at seducing a company of priests who hithertofore have lived pure lives of service to the Lord. Unfortunately for Greed, at the last minute, Reason, which Prudentius calls "the guardian of the tribe of Levi," comes to the rescue and saves all but a few of them.[29] Having been thus temporarily thwarted, Greed flies into a rage, delivering one of the most vituperative diatribes in Western literature. Once her screed is done, and vowing that what she cannot conquer by force, she will most assuredly capture by subterfuge, Greed changes her approach and feigns a certain nobility of character.

Laying her weapons down, she changes her robes and her demeanor to ones of simple austerity and becomes, Prudentius says, "the virtue that men know as Thrift." As Thrift, Greed manages to control, or at least to hide, all of her grasping and rage, and instead takes up what the poet calls, "the delicate veil of maternal concern," claiming that all her miserliness and hoarding—even perhaps just a bit of her cheating—are done in the praise worthy name of providing for her children.[30] The human souls within her range of influence, we are told, begin to follow Greed's instructions and ways, thinking that her work is one of virtue, not vice; and thus, Prudentius says, "The wicked fiend finds them cheerful victims happy to live in her shackles."[31]

And so it goes until Good Works, in a somewhat anticlimactic conclusion to so much storm and stress, at last drives Greed away. But what matters out of all this very physical contest is that the *Psychomachia* is the story that established at a popular level Greed's sex, her image as mother of a deadly clan, her worrisome ability to change into false virtue upon demand, and more suggested than stated, the understanding that greed is actually the sin of apostasy, of desiring a life subject to human control over a life of vulnerable trust in the unseen.[32]

Despite the fact that the long centuries of the Middle Ages, both early and late, had embraced Prudentius's conventions as being the truth about greed,[33] the Renaissance still came along and the Reformation evolved and the seat of the Western imagination shifted. In that strange century of transition from one way of being to the next, two painters, fellow countrymen, caught greed's progress across the disconnect better than any verbal commentary ever could have.

Hieronymus Bosch (ca. 1450–1516) was absorbed with sin his entire life (as are most of us, but his was a professional as well as a personal absorption). Much of Bosch's study of sin is orthodox, at least in its theology, despite the fact that little else in Bosch usually is. His most renowned treatment of sin is his *The Seven Deadly Sins*, which was commissioned by Philip II and still hangs in El Prado. Arranged as a circle of seven, pie-shaped wedges, the canvas shows in the center of the circle at the apex of each of the seven wedges, the all-seeing eye of God. In each wedge, a human enactment of a specific sin is dramatically portrayed. Avarice's vignette is of a corrupt judge who is shown receiving a bribe with one hand even as he rules against a supplicant with the other, all very much as we would expect. It is, instead, in his *The Haywain* that we come to fully appreciate Bosch's involvement with greed as well as its centrality for him as he struggled to redefine the scheme of this world's ways and woes.

A triptych, *The Haywain* in its left panel, depicts the expulsion of both the rebellious angels from Heaven and of Adam and Eve from Eden; in the right is hell itself in all its lurid detail. In the large center panel is a troupe of all sorts and conditions of humankind making their way from Eden behind them to the inferno ahead. The dominant image in this center panel of progression is of a giant hay wagon, or haywain, atop which in mixed array sit the beauties and the horrors of sin—wealth, handsome costumes, murder, lovely objects, deceit, distortion. As the haywain trucks its way across a fairly traditional landscape, it grinds beneath its wheels all the men and women in its path, most of whom are greedily looking up and futilely grasping at the hay for a purchase to its top. There is no battle here, no contest, but there is a huge appeal to reason; and there is as well an innovation of approach that presents sin at a remove, thus giving us perspective by means of its very distance. There is, in other words, the foreshadowing of a more intellectualized approach to the business of sin in general and especially of greed in particular.

Pieter Bruegel the Elder (ca. 1525–1569), coming just slightly after Bosch, dances the same dance between old and new, but to even more dramatic effect. In 1556, only forty years after Bosch's death, Bruegel produced two works on greed. The first was one piece in a study of the seven deadlies in which Avarice is shown as a regal queen of rapacious demeanor and ample skirts who commands an army of chimera. Human guards with the beaks of greedy birds pour coins from cracked jardinieres into overflowing coffers while humanized ghouls, bald headed and pie eyed, languish in a landscape of thorn thickets. While hardly standard stuff—it is Bruegel, after all—still there is little here to herald any impending and deep rifts in the West's conceptualization of greed as a mortal sin to be opposed at all costs.

The second of the two works done in 1557 is a different matter entirely. It is the engraving titled *Big Fish Eat Little Fish* and is as clearly predictive of Charles Darwin as to have been his prime inspiration and first instructor. Although we like to forget it nowadays, the truth is that Darwinism and nineteenth-century scholarship, when they at last did come, were driven by a good deal more than what we today would regard as pure scientific objectivity. They were, in point of fact, driven just as much, if not more, by the eighteenth century's Enlightenment need to reconcile belief in a benevolent God with the realities of a deeply flawed and besmirched creation of the very kind that Bruegel the Elder depicted. Scholarly thinking in the early nineteenth century sought, that is, to push the origins of evil as far away as possible from traditional, largely theological tales of their genesis.[34]

Bruegel's prophetic study, then, is of a beached fish so massive that one fisherman must use a ladder to mount its back while another uses a knife longer than he himself is to cut into the creature's abdominal cavity. Out of that great wound pour myriad other sea creatures, while likewise from the carcass's mouth pour dozens of other fish, several of them in their death throes and vomiting forth even smaller fish from their own sizeable maws.[35]

There is in all this macabre rendering not one whiff of either emotion or theology, only a neutral observation of the way things really are, along with a kind of tacit acceptance of the acceptability of that position. Indeed, squatting noncommitally on a nearby bank, another fisherman is calmly using a small fish to entice a larger one to strike his hook. Such existential sangfroid is, we recognize instantly, much more comfortable for us than Pruden-tius's warfare ever could be, primarily because it is infinitely closer to us in its reformative objectivity.

The Reformation stands as the most dramatic example in the Christian West of a disjuncture between how things are observed to be and the received understanding of why they are. We speak of this bloody time of disconnect with a capital "R" and the tacit assumption that it is a discrete period of history that conveniently dates from an October morning in 1517, when a young priest tacked the tenets of a new world order on the door of his church in Wittenberg, and ends with the advent of the age of reason. While the capital "R" Reformation may indeed be a definable period, the spirit of re-formation or reformation with a lower case "r" was to be the evolving zeitgeist that informed the next 400 plus years and integrated them into an intelligible whole. Fifteen hundred years of trying to wrestle a new religion into mature, manageable shape had laid the accretion of 1,500 years of vested interests on the story, the burden of the faithfuls' attention having been more on the integrity of the body of belief—i.e., its corporeality—than on its originating genius.

What died at Wittenberg and what was birthed there differ at an applied level in myriad and sometimes minor ways, but they also differ at their very core. What died was Olympian, what came was urban. The former imagined itself in terms of Zion and the mighty hills, the latter in terms of the town square.[36] Alexander Pope, writing from the perspective of the eighteenth century and the remove of some two centuries, probably furnishes us the most pregnant, if overcited, summary of the shift when he declared that humanity itself was the proper study for humanity.[37]

Through the narrows of "humanity as the first duty of the text in all things" would walk not only Protestantism but its legitimate daughter of capitalism; the perceived duality of mind and body; the temporary death of metaphysics; the notion of a *tabula rasa*; the physical and experimental sciences of first the cosmos and ultimately of the atom as well as of chaos; the beginning of the democratization of information; the trenchant, if ultimately transient, supremacy of the printed word over the visual image; the political and social origins of authority; the working premise of the individuality of the soul and the individuation of moral responsibility together with the social nature of its definitions; socialism and communism; the increased hegemony of philosophy and reason in the determination of good and with it the noble savage; the behavioral sciences and situational standards for explaining and monitoring human conduct.

This list too is essentially as inexhaustible as the making of it is foolhardy, because each member part of it splinters immediately upon its being named into dozens more sequellae. For our purposes here, however, the shift of greatest consequence snaked its way—to use a freighted image—into the sleeve of the common imagination rather than besieging it. Under the rush to autonomy and the deluge of reason that followed it in the late eighteenth and the nineteenth centuries, greed gradually ceased to be imagined as an issue of sin and damnation,[38] and came instead to be understood, a distinction that made all the difference in how greed was to be engaged.

Indeed, by the end of the last century, psychology and its related sciences had developed a veritable panoply of theoretical constructs, schools of analysis, and therapeutic methodologies. Most of them were dedicated to improving human well-being, and almost all of them were also predicated upon the assumption that greed and any other of the so-called sins or vices are not so much free-standing evils as they are haunting—and here I quote Professor Solomon Schimmel of Hebrew College—"relics of antiquated theological and philosophical traditions, which it [i.e., psychology] has superseded."[39] Many who comment upon our times and condition, be they lay or professional, now share Professor Schimmel's somewhat arch assessment of where this tack, if accepted uncritically, can lead—and indeed has led—human well-being.

Assigning the origin of evil either to biological process or, by extension, to psychological process makes human beings the victims of process. As such, it demands the attitudes and creates the depression and resentments of impotency that are the characteristics of victimization. Under these circumstances, "feeling good" or, less colloquially, achieving a state of perceived internal balance, becomes an attractive and powerful definition of good; but by the very nature of its parameters, such a goal is individualized in definition and isolating in its progress.

Referred to by Schimmel as the "secularization of evil," this shift from divinity or divine machinations to physical cause-and-effect as the source of our destructive and flawed natures has had an even more demeaning, and sometimes flagrantly neurotic, consequence over the last century and a half. It has robbed Western citizenry, to some greater or lesser extent, of the energizing and focusing dignity of spiritual struggle by robbing us of faith in the eventual benevolence of how things are. The secularization of evil, that is, makes human beings objects and not participants in creation. It assumes as well an immutability or impersonality of conditions and principles that blocks us from hope. In its defense, such thinking may lead us to compassion. Certainly we have seen that shift occur in American culture rather dramatically over the last forty or so years. But compassion built on a mind-set of "fellow prisoners together" is just that—compassion, not love; evolved rather than forged; in its origin more a creature of situation than of grace.

As a result, the first thing third-millennium thought should confess about greed, other than acknowledging her colorful history, is that regardless of whether we are theological or secular in our particular world view, issues of meaning or nonmeaning with their concomitant values and explanations are operational the instant we begin to engage her. As the simile of the anchoring rope has suggested from time in memorium, the engagement of greed is, of necessity a religious matter, even if the religion involved be secularism.[40] Many of us in my line of business would also add, even emphasize, as does Professor Schimmel himself, that it is the responsibility of theistic religion, "to translate its relevant teachings [i.e., about greed] into an idiom that speaks to modern man while respecting his skepticism about religious dogma."[41]

And because Professor Schimmel wrote those words some ten years ago, I would add—I even suspect he would join me in adding—that the greater concern today for the theistic faiths must be for postmodern humankind and for the imminent, arduous business of discovering a new shared imagination as well as new applications and appreciation for our story, a matter that this essay will shortly address by image rather than words.

Be all that as it may, the several streams of Western Christianity that emerged intact from the Reformation, while they differed among themselves in the nuances of their various dogmas, in the main agreed in their adherence to the doctrine of original sin and greed as a prime evidence thereof. The tenet that sin, for whatever reason, entered the human constitution with the fall of Adam and that opposing it had been the human struggle ever since was, as a result, a solid part of the theology that came out of the old ways and into the new. Within a century, however, Thomas Hobbes (1588–1679) would persuade that it is the social contract—the collective group—that is empowered to define sin. And within less than another century, Rousseau and the Enlightenment would reject original sin as implausible. In the course of that progression, sin and greed as a major presentation of it ceased to be exclusively religious issues, becoming instead matters of moral concern in mainstream Western thought, just as within the subset of conservative thought they increasingly remained religious by extension from morality.[42]

After Bruegel, then, and with the obvious exception of John Milton,[43] over the first centuries of the intellectual imagination, there are few "pictures" per se for us to reference when we speak of greed. Rather, the focus of all the energy of discovery about her moved from the domain of spiritual warfare into the domain of moral knowing; and greed, over those decades, drifts slowly from personified sin to moral theory—epistemological, political, economic, and social moral theory. As in the *Psychomachia,* where Greed changed her name from *avaritia* to those of Thrift and maternal concern in order to address new challenges, so here again did Greed adopt names that were—that, in fact, still are— seductive and coy, names like laissez faire, the social contract, imminent domain, the wealth of nations, free trade, industrious- ness. The litany is again a long one, just as the conversations the names evoke became secularized in direct proportion to the degree of their removal from the immediately physical.

Such pictures as did appertain in the seventeenth and eighteenth centuries, however, were in the main a thin gruel, more caricature than picture, quick studies with immediate not eternal messages. When visual, they were more often than not cartoons that presented their greedy subjects as blotches on the common good rather than as the subjects of hell's fire. Not infrequently the later, more subtle works of the Enlightenment and of Romanticism sought to blame not so much greed's human hosts as the circumstances that had militated for, or resulted in, her activity among them.

Near the coming of modernity, we capture that process quite tellingly in British literature[44] where in George Eliot's *Silas Marner*, for instance, we have an exquisitely crafted, albeit romantic and sympathetic, presentation of the latter approach. That is, it is the tragedy of social and religious circumstance, not personal failing, that brings the old weaver of Raveloe to the exercise of an excoriating greed; just as it is the almost accidental grace of an abandoned baby that rescues him from his hell on earth. Likewise, in Dickens's *A Christmas Carol* we see the literary edition of a man who is more a caricature in a cautionary tale than a creation of classic genius. Indeed, Scrooge is so completely a caricature that he is better known to thousands of school children today as a duck than as a human being.

The arrival of modernity has been assigned several dates, the most defensible of which—occurring only about twenty-five years after Scrooge—is, I believe, 1882. That is the year when Nietzsche announced that God was dead. God was and God wasn't, of course; for what Nietzsche remarked in his announcement was not so much a death as the completion of an extreme transposition. What had died was conservative resistance to the thesis that the Western intellect was the accepted center for considering the Absolute. For Nietzsche, having at last been given such certification, human intelligence was both the absolute itself and the final freedom—except, of course, that his was a Pyrrhic victory of sorts. Nietzsche couldn't quite shuck life itself off the cob of his joy, and he finally had to accept as the—or an—absolute that life itself exists. The only way for him to deal with this inelegance finally was to accept its eternal recurrence and then usurp power over it.

In this usurpation, three things, Nietzsche said—three forces, if you will—would be necessary: greed, envy, and hatred, in that order. What had begun as an opponent in a battle for the souls of humanity and had then become a factor in a struggle for the well-being of humanity would now become a potent tool in the perfecting of humanity.[45]

Nietzsche would also say that whatever else the world might say in time of him, it would say as well that Friedrich Nietzsche had been a part of something tremendous in a time of crisis without equal. He was right on both counts. The next eleven decades would be ones of the wild, unfettered pursuit of power; and as the generator to the motor, so greed-as-force to power-as-goal. Our own time in the common era had begun; and the trajectory from Adam Smith to Ayn Rand to Arthur Andersen had been irreversibly plotted.[46]

The new period of modernity may have organized around the pursuit of power; but the mind that informed that pursuit, discovering itself to indeed be free at last, quickly found that it was also free to explore its own inadequacy. Nietzsche was right that life went on, but Søren Kierkegaard was right in saying that if it were to, then there must be meaning. A new God was being born—or a new imagination that wanted images for pondering such an existential God; and since the images of an earlier imagination were the place where Western culture had last enjoyed a source of personal meaning with any kind of familiarity to it, they became the places to begin to look for what was to be.

The Belgian painter James Ensor—Baron Ensor—produced his masterpieces primarily in the first two decades of modernity—that is, in the last two decades of the nineteenth century. Working under the imperative of new paths out of old roads, Ensor returned to the bizarre and powerful landscapes and imagery of Bosch and Bruegel for instruction. In terms of aesthetic history as a cultural discipline, Ensor's re-employment of those themes would open the door to surrealism, thereby enabling a conversation of distortion that could at last address the ethereal beauty and horror of power. Of particular interest to us here, however, is the fact that as part of his struggle toward a new language, Ensor returned to the seven deadly sins. He renders them as grotesqueries that, in their conceptualization, are more reminiscent of the Baron's mentors than they are prescient; but by rendering them, Ensor returned the seven deadly sins to their proper place as subjects for serious visual and literary discourse within a time of transition

Ensor's rendering of greed—a fearsome skeleton of a creature sitting at a counting table on which perches a Greco-Roman harpy just waiting to torment, while in the background another creature holds an ax poised at the counting miser's neck and a dreadful dwarf prods him unceasingly with a dagger from the side—is not far beyond Bosch's, in other words; but it was sufficiently so to be predictive as well as influential.

There is no question but that Ensor returned the imaging of sin and greed to their former place as fit subjects for the visual arts in the new century.[47] Beyond that, however, Ensor's handling of sin deals in terms suggestive of the pseudo- or neo-medievalism that informed some of the twentieth century's more memorable treatments of not only sin but also religion in general. In this regard, one thinks immediately of Otto Dix's startling, garish, masterful mixed media procession of the seven deadly sins. Fundamentally medieval in image and narrative, Dix's scathing condemnation of Nazi morality, with its caricature of Hitler as Envy, caught as well the growing popular sense of greed as someone else's sin and/or as the sin of the oppressor.[48]

The same idea was carried over as well for use in modernity's preferred new visual medium of celluloid, where it held pride of place for several decades as the proper interpretation of greed. One of the classic films of all time, still venerated today as a masterpiece by historians and connoisseurs alike, is Erich von Stroheim's 1923 proletariat-championing *Greed*, a cinematic treatment of Frank Norris's 1899 novel *McTeague: A Story of San Francisco*. Even Gordon Gekko's brilliant paean to rampant greed in the 1987 film *Wall Street* stays, by and large, within the same interpretive perspective.[49] And these are the artifacts our great-great-grandchildren will understand us by, discovering in them most certainly the records not so much of sinners as of citizens disenfranchised by greed.[50] Certainly in the decades of Michael Milken and trickle-down economics, we ourselves did not note our state as the disenfranchised with any alarm; we were enjoying the ride too much—we were, that is, until right up to the fall of 2001. And what a ride.

"Billionaire" as a means for defining the extent of vast wealth varies, naturally, as a real measure with the changing value of currency. To compensate for these fluctuations, the Gross Domestic Product is employed as a standard of measure. The private fortunes of any given decade are assessed in terms of the GDP for the decade in which they occur. Thus, two more images, also pictorial in their own way, for they are drawn from economics, a primary art form in modernity.[51] The first image is this: in 1998 a billion dollars was the total lifetime output of 20,000 American workers; and every billionaire absorbed the entire cradle-to-grave productive life of another 20,000 of his fellow citizens every time he grew his own fortune by another billion.

Second, in 1982, as Euro-America recovered from the Great Depression and from, among other things, three major wars, there were in the United States twenty-three billionaires. In 1996—fourteen years later—there were well over five times that many. That is, there were 132 billionaires in the United States. It was during that fourteen years that Gordon Gekko spoke his paean. Theater audiences may have thought Michael Douglas was merely enacting an exaggerated role, but he wasn't; and collusion of ordinary citizens—our guilt, if you will—in the whole thing is no different from Martha Stewart's or Bernie Ebbers's or Jack Welch's or even the NBA players', for that matter. We differ from them, most of us, only in degree, not in intention.

Yet while in America our hands were occupied counting our phantom money—on which ironically we have always struck the motto of "In God We Trust"—the religion institutionalized by the Western intellectual imagination was collapsing just as surely as the religion institutionalized by the physical imagination had done some 400-plus years before. Once again the sheer weight of political greed would first stifle and then smother an ecclesial system. So too would a possessive inability to release sacred story to any exegesis other than the established and enfranchised one; and so too would an avaritious clergy, or an ubiquitous simony.[52] Simony is, of course, a basically Roman term for what alas has presented to us in modernity not as colorful Chaucerian pardoners but as evangelists and, especially, as televangelists—every one of whom is so easy to spoof and deride that they and, more importantly, the constructs behind them have gradually been rendered not so much vile as pathetic in our general conversation.

All of which is to say that the symptoms and causes of the Reformation differ from the symptoms and causes of our recent disconnect more in wrappings than in content, the motto of the former—the priesthood of all believers—being remarkably like the motto of ours—I'm spiritual but not religious—which, truth being told, is a bit like saying, "I'm human, but not flesh and bones." My suspicion, though, is that the work of transitioning, which is patent in the popular origins of that thirty-year-old expression of "I'm spiritual but not religious," reached a kind of turning point or completion during the months after the bombing of the World Trade Towers. Insensitive and impolitic as it may seem to say so, the fact still is that 9/11, which was itself both the work and the result of greed, inestimably accelerated the process of popular change into a new way of being; and history, unless I am very, very wrong, will assign 9/11 a specificity of dating much like that struck into our cultural calendar by the blows of Luther's hammer on the doors of Wittenberg.

What, then, can we say of this new time, this next era whose advent we have half-articulated for little more than a quarter-century and which we now suspect may have been at work among us for four times that long? How shall we define it? How enter it? How conceive of sin—of greed and all her children—in it? One last image.

Being Another Prologue

Mario Donizetti, the great Italian realist and polymath, will be remembered as our DaVinci. More than any other contemporary Western visualist, Donizetti has understood that new imagination must always go back to ask from its ancients the footings for its own work. Saying that destruction of the past leads to silence, Donizetti teaches that what must come next is a reverence for whatever is left standing out of what has been. For Donizetti, the giant left standing in a time of greed will always be Dante, and it was Dante whom he began to engage some thirty years ago. Though the intellectual affinity between the dead poet and the living painter has ranged over much of Western thought, it was within Dante's treatment of the seven deadly sins that some fifteen or twenty years ago Donizetti found the wellspring for his definitive masterpiece.

As his preparatory study of, and absorption with, the sins increased, so too did Donizetti's obsessive concern with the colors and hues required for translating the seven deadly sins over into the tongue of the emerging new zeitgeist. Convinced that only the luminosity and transparency of pastels would be semantically sufficient, but aware that that medium has always had the limitations of transience and fading, he struggled for several years to effect a new way of painting and what he now calls a new chromatism. In the last decade of the last century, Donizetti finally perfected a new pastel technique involving fundamental modifications in both the traditional structure and the methods of that medium. The first innovation was to substitute for paper a canvas glued onto a board with a preparation made of finely ground Carrara marble and reversible glue. The second adaptation was to fix the pigment to the new kind of canvas by exposing it for an extended period to boiling steam until such time as pastel, canvas, glue, and marble were no longer four, but one. The resulting surface, so completely bonded that it may be glazed time and time again, even varnished or have new pigment laid over it, has, as Donizetti himself observes, "the classic transparency and shading of the best egg tempera painting" with the permanence of canvas.[53]

Donizetti's *Seven Deadly Sins* are a suite of seven panels. Four of the panels run on horizontal axis and three on a vertical one. When the pieces are shown in reproduction as an assemblage, two horizontals are at the top and two at the bottom with the three verticals upright in the midsection separating the horizontal rows. Among the three verticals, avarice occupies the middle position, and therefore the center of the assemblage, in recognition of her traditional place.[54]

There is a certain disorientation present in looking at Donizetti's avarice. There is, eerily, no longer any proscenium effect, no sense of someone "other" whom we are watching. Rather, her short, curly, sensuously tousled hair and her large brown eyes are us; and we dumbly know what they feel like, for we or others whom we treasure have them as well. Our fingers have known the feel of that hair and our eyes have seen the deep awareness in hers.

There are neither clothes nor artifices to distract the viewer or give some purchase of interpretation, for she is naked and we move into her whether we will it or not. Painted with breasts but without her sex, she sits, instead, astride a lumpy, tight-cinched tow sack and holds another, smaller one up against her sad young face as if to pillow her head there. In her anxiety, she has pulled herself and her sacks off the ground and onto a low marble platform barely large enough to protect her; while at her feet the skeletal remains of poverty seem to be struggling out to pull her to them even as she cowers, pathetic and beautiful, on her lumpy bag and inadequate pedestal. Behind her, there is not a geographic landscape, but a nonlocative one of the dark, yet luminous colors we recognize immediately as those we inhabit when in prayer or meditation.

This, then, is Donizetti's avarice who has crossed over out of life and begun to shrink into herself. The stark agony of her existence, like a single column, half-broken and with its capital gone, stands tragic and eternal, as if on some verge where a pebbled clearing touches an engulfing woods. To look is to ache.

I spoke in the beginning of the long lens of history as a corrective to too-quick judgment as well as a relief to daunting angst, and for me that is so; for when I look through the last 2,000 years, I see at each turn of the road, each change of perception, each repositioning of attention, that it has been greed and her children who have whipped or frightened or cajoled or tricked us to this place—this place of Donizetti's where, the smoke of the soul's battle and the bold colors of deliberated progress having cleared, there is, exposed before us, the numinous spirit, elegant and trembling in its death.

Through the mouth of the prophet Isaiah, the Lord God says: "I am the Lord, and there is none else. I form the light, and create darkness: I make peace, and create evil: I the Lord do all these things."[55]

Such knowledge is too wonderful for me; but when Donizetti paints for us, I understand that, though still beyond the reach of all naming, such mystery probably is the next imagination for most of us who have joined one another here in these pages; and I pray God this will be the one that makes us whole.

Notes

1. These shifts and disjunctions are hardly limited to religion in their influence and impact. The Hungarian-born and now American historian John Lukacs, in his *At the End of an Age* (New Haven: Yale University Press, 2002), brilliantly exposes and interprets the secular as well as religious implications and repercussions of the closing of the modern era (by which he means roughly the 500 years since the end of the Middle Ages). Readers interested in pursuing the economic, social, philosophic, and political ramifications of living "at the end of an age" could not find a better guide to them than Lukacs's book by the same name.

2. Space in the present context permits only the most abbreviated summary of these cultural shifts and their theological and ecclesial sequellae. Interested readers will find a more comprehensive treatment of them in my *God-Talk in America* (New York: Crossroad Publishers, 1997).

3. New York: HarperCollins, 1995.

4. New York: Palgrave/St. Martin's Press, 2001.

   In citing Watson and Portmann, I have of course cited examples of nonfiction titles. This does not for one minute mean that to be successful in the treatment of sin and greed millennial-era titles have had to fall within that category. My own journal, for instance, gave its highest encomium of a starred reviews in 2002 to *All I Could Get* by Scott Lasser

(New York: Alfred A. Knopf, 2002), and Kate Jennings, *Moral Hazard* (New York: Fourth Estate, 2002), both of them novels and both of them, again as their titles would suggest, dealing solely with sin, particularly greed.

5. Nor were Oxford and the New York Public Library alone in this. Boston University, some months earlier, invited Joyce Carol Oates, Kathleen Norris, and Nathan Englander to present similar public papers on evil, thereby evoking a good deal of popular and media conversation themselves.

6. Compare Fairlie, *The Seven Deadly Sins* (Notre Dame: University of Notre Dame Press, 1995) and following. As Fairlie notes, over its 2,000 years of Western hegemony, Christian theology and culture have managed to imagine sin with a skill and finesse that approach a fine art and that have resulted in what some scholars now refer to as the "spiritualization of vice." Thus, preoccupation with sin was the theological, if not the cultural, economic, or ecclesial, impetus behind the Protestant Reformation; and one has only to look at the great names of nascent and early Protestantism to be reminded of this. From Luther with his ink pot and his Devil to Cotton Mather to Jerry Falwell is a fairly straight, if ever less appealing, progression. Among the less raucous and less assertive, however, an abiding concern for an understanding of sin and a release from its dominion is just as consistently present, infusing my communion with an intensity of private analysis and a conscious dependency on grace that, in the devout, has become the soft, sweet patina of the church on earth.

7. The most imaginative and perhaps the kindest explanation

of greed that follows this line of reasoning comes from Judaism, which postulates the presence in each of us of the *yetzer hara*, or evil drive, which in the case of greed, my friend and instructor in such matters, Dr. Robert Rabinowitz of the National Jewish Center for Learning and Leadership, defines colloquially as the "constant clamoring of the acquisitive drive within us for more 'stuff.'" The "stuff," by the way, he defines as being "more power, more money, and higher social status, etc., etc."(Compare "The SEC as Spiritual Apparatus," *e-CLAL*, the webzine of CLAL, July 2002.) *Y tz'r*, the Hebrew root from which *yetzer* derives, is used in the Genesis story, along with *asah* and *bara*, to mean "He created." The difference between *yatzer* and *bara* is that *bara* refers to *creatio ex nihilo*, whereas *yetzer* means to form something out of existing matter. It is an informing subtlety, for in it we find, set like a perfect jewel, one of the great distinguishing questions *intra familia* among the Abrahamic faiths and their dependent bodies about Greed. Thus, Dr. Rabinowitz glosses for us, ". . . *yetzer* is not just will—but the inclination to create" (from an e-letter to the author, 13 August 2002).

8. The use of seven for numbering the significant pieces and parts of life is apparently as old as humankind's ability either to count or to strain toward objective representations of perfection. Within the Abrahamic faiths, the first occurrence of the use of seven for numbering humanity's offenses against God can be found in Proverbs 6: 16–19: "There are six things that the Lord hates, seven that are an abomination to him" (*NRSV*) In the Roman literature of the axial era,

moreover, we find Horace's first epistle, which dates from ca. 20 B.C.E., listing the seven deadly sins in a presentation that we would recognize today: *avaritia, laudis amor, invidus, iracundus, iners, vinosus, amator* (covetousness, love of praise, envy, anger, sloth, gluttony, lust). Though Horace's work is nondoctrinal from an Abrahamic or even theistic point of view, it is within the mainstream of Epicureanism; and as an Epicurean, Horace regarded the excesses of these seven vices as threats to the *ataraxia* or serenity, which was the *summum bonum* (highest good) of his school of philosophy. (For more on this and related matters, the reader may wish to see Paul Jordan-Smith, "Seven [and More] Deadly Sins," *Parabola*, vol. 10, no. 4 (1985): 34–45.)

We should also note here, albeit briefly, that during the first heyday of Christianity's almost neurotic absorption with sin and its divisions, eight sins or vices were recognized. John Cassian (ca. 360–435), a Rumanian Christian monk credited with carrying into Western Christianity many of the increasingly signatory particularities of Eastern Christianity, became the authority for an octad, as well as the first to give it broad credence. Richard Newhauser, the contemporary authority without equal on the history of greed, argues persuasively that it was Cassian's penetrating analyses of greed that led him to elevate to fuller stature acts and attitudes that had previously been regarded only as derivative or spawns of avarice (*The Early History of Greed: The Sin of Avarice in Early Medieval Thought and Literature* [Cambridge: Cambridge University Press, 2000], 110–111) The eight as Cassian and others rendered them were: gluttony, fornication, avarice, anger, dejection, sloth, vainglory, and pride.

9. "The terms *vice* and *sin* are often interchanged in medieval writings, but they are not identical. Vices and virtues were the concepts and terms of Greek and Roman philosophers; sin of the Hebrew Bible and New Testament. Vices are character traits. Sins are specific acts of commission or omission." Solomon Schimmel, *The Seven Deadly Sins: Jewish, Christian, and Classical Reflections on Human Psychology* (New York: Oxford University Press, 1997), 14.

10. While others may argue or even deplore the conflation of act with thought, it is neither a caprice of Christian theologians nor a position open to negotiation for believers, since it is based on some of the clearest, least debatable sections of Christian scripture. For example and famously, Jesus, when speaking about adultery, said: "You have heard that it was said, 'You shall not commit adultery.' But I say to you that everyone who looks at a woman with lust has already committed adultery with her in his heart" (Matt. 6:27, 28 *NRSV*).

11. This early perception of covetousness or greed as source, rather than substance, of sin has continued to inform Judaism. David Noel Freedman, in his influential *The Nine Commandments* (New York: Doubleday, 2000), 155, for example, argues that effectively speaking, there are only nine commandments instead of the generally accepted ten, because the last of Sinai's injunctions, "Thou shalt not covet your neighbor's house," and "Thou shalt not covet your neighbor's wife, or his male servant or his female servant, or his ox, or his donkey, or

anything that belongs to your neighbor" does not name a sin, but forbids an attitude. To be specific, the last of Sinai's words, *covetousness*, is "in violation of God's will, but it is not in violation of Israelite law."

12. Long before English indulged in such a glut of terminology, Greek and Latin, the languages that undergirded the intellectual and ecclesial evolution of modern European thought, likewise indulged it. The New Testament employs πλεονεξίαι (compare Mark 7:22) for what is usually translated as "covetousness" or "covetous desires." Φιλάργυροι (compare Luke 16:14) names those who love money, or its other noun form, φιλαργυρία (compare 1 Tim. 6:10), names the sin itself, literally "the love of silver." The writer of the epistle to the Romans used επιθυμία or variants of it (compare Rom.7:7;13:9) for covetousness. The most contested term in New Testament Greek, however, is probably αίσχροκερδής, an adjective conveying the idea of seeking or desiring dishonest gain (compare 1 Tim. 3:8). It and its cognates—the adverb αίσχροκερδῶς, for example (1 Pet. 5:2)—are omitted from some texts.

The Latin of the church fathers employed φιλαργυρία, the Greek idea of the love of silver, extensively, but they transliterated it variously as *filargiria, philargyria,* or *philargiria. Avaritia,* however, was probably as widely used, as was *cupiditas.*

Each of these names for greed in whatever Indo-European lexicon offers some slight shading of nuance, but with the possible exception of "simony " or the distinction between "avarice" and "covetousness," greed's many names are at a practical level little more than sobriquets devolving from a funereal theme. As is often the case when more labels than genuine distinctions abound in a taxonomy, the true difficulty with greed arises from the lack of a clear, adequate, and descriptive definition of the thing being named. With this problem, Islam can be of great assistance to us, for Islam defines greed pictorially, a method that I will employ extensively in the body of this essay.

Greed, according to the Prophet, is having or desiring anything more than what is required of a man in order—and I quote—in order "to keep his back straight." It is a holy wording that I find to be as lovely as it is capacious and utile. The most complete treatment of greed in this regard with which I am familiar is *Dealing with Lust and Greed According to Islam* by Sheikh 'Abd al-Hamid Kishk (London: Dar Al Taqawa, Ltd., 1995). Readers will find there that the use of the image of keeping one's back straight as a defining principle commences on page 34 and threads its way like a leitmotif through the rest of the book's argument.

13. Mr. Greenspan made his widely reported and now-famous comments on greed and avarice in his semiannual report on the economy to the Senate Banking Committee on 16 July 2002. The next morning, the *New York Times* ran, as its front-page lead, coverage of what it termed, "Mr. Greenspan's blunt testimony to Congress about avarice in the executive suite."

14. Tim. 6:10.

15. We must remember in all of this, however, that in Christianity's opening decades, matters of greed were less culturally

and politically muddled than they were later and/or are today for several reasons. Consequently, Paul's concept of greed as the source of all evil made perfect historical and contextual, as well as theological, sense. First-century Judaism, of which the church was still an irregular but empathetic part, was bombarded at every turn by concerns about wealth, property, and ownership.

From its earliest days, Judaism had developed laws governing the ownership of land that were distinct from those governing the possession of other forms of wealth. Jewish law even prohibited the Levitical priesthood from having a land allotment or inheritance within Israel for, says the Torah, "the Lord is their inheritance" (Deut. 18:1–5). The implication clearly is that such ownership would compromise the purity and focus of the Levites in their holy duties. (It should be noted, however, that this ideal did not survive the deprivations and social changes that attended the Jews' return from the Babylonian Captivity. We read in Nehemiah, for instance, that certain priests owned fields; and by the time of Josephus, a wealthy, land-owning priest was not even an unusual priest.)

Alongside the entrenched concept in early Judaism of freedom from possession as a spiritual strength was the equally entrenched concept of the land as different from other forms of life's goods. "The land," God says in Lev. 25:23, "shall not be sold in perpetuity, for the land is mine; with me you are but aliens and tenants" (*NRSV*). Because the land, unlike other possessible "things," was life, it was reasonable as well as divinely decreed that it should lie beyond the reach of permanent human ownership; and on this one fundamental principle, John Dominic Crossan, Jesus scholar and professor emeritus of De Paul University, reminds us, hung a good deal of Jewish law and a very great deal of first-century Judaism's abhorrence of Rome as well as its assessment of Rome as infinitely greedy.

"If the land could not be bought and sold like any other commodity," Professor Crossan writes, "then neither could it be mortgaged and dispossessed. Hence all those laws about the forbidding of interest and the controlling of collateral, the remission of debts and the liberation of enslavement every seventh, or Sabbath year, and the reversal of dispossession every fiftieth, or Jubilee, year." And, he continues, "such covenantal laws would have seemed like bad jokes to the Roman conquerors, in whose eyes the land belonged to them, or, if one wished to wax theological about it, to Jupiter now and to Yahweh no longer. . . . It is that fundamental clash . . . that explains the terrible failure of Roman policy. . . . Three rebellions there, in 4 B.C.E., in 66–74 C.E., and in 132–35 C.E. . . . emphasize that failure." (*Excavating Jesus* [San Francisco: HarperSanFrancisco, 2001], 273, 274.)

It was into this set of multiple tensions and circumstances and this complex of religious values that the Christian Church was born, and out of them that it began to operate. It should come as no surprise, then, that the first Christian ecclesial court of which we know anything at all was an adjudication of sorts involving the ownership of land and greed over its proceeds. Two early converts, Ananias and his wife, Sapphira, owned a piece of land that they sold as a means of supporting the young Christian community. That was as it should have been. The error was that while they claimed before the whole body that they had brought in the entire sum realized from the sale of their land, they had in actuality kept back a portion for themselves. Challenged individually by Saint Peter to change their story and admit their greed, both denied having contributed less than the entire sales price. Peter condemns their duplicity with the result that both Ananias and Sapphira instantly drop dead at his feet.

16. My Italian-born son-in-law would have me add just here that there is yet another image from pre-Reformation ecclesia that is both more colorful and more lasting. It comes from the work of Saint Boniface, that wily and evangelizing old Anglo-Saxon who labored in many vineyards during the first half of the eighth century and ended up as a patron saint of Germany for his trouble. According to Boniface, greed was the most unholy of beginnings. Not generated according to any laws of God or nature, she instead was delivered out of the bowels of the serpent in the Garden of Eden after Adam and Eve were expelled from that place. In *Cupiditas*, his definitive work on the subject, Boniface admittedly does little more than record the artifices of medieval Christian society's very physical imagination, but he does revel more than the fastidious might in some of his tale's elaborations. Thus Boniface envisions greed or cupidity as having inherited the fangs, the "serpent teeth," of her progenitor and as having, in her full maturity, the unattractive habit of bragging constantly about the thousands of our kind whom

she has sent to hell's fires with her prodigious and venomous bite. This image, according to the son-in-law, is the basis of one of the rhetorical staples of his own boyhood decades ago where he was routinely told, *"La moneta e il merde del diavolo,"* "Money is the feces sh[–] of the devil," and *"Quando il diavolo de tentare con moneta, lui te manga la tua anima. Doppo, quando lui se cacce, se cacca pui moneta,"* "When the devil tempts you, he uses money. After he has consumed your soul, he defecates more money."

17. One sees much the same kind of caustic commentary today in acrostics like:

> *U*nited in the
> *S*tates of
> *A*varice.

18. In this regard, see in particular chapter 29 of *De spectaculis.*

19. S. Georgia Nugent, *"Virtus* or Virago? The Female Personifications of Prudentius's *Psychomachia,"* in *Virtue and Vice– The Personifications in the Index of Christian Art,* ed. Colum Hourihane (Princeton: Princeton University Press, 2000), 13.

20. It should be noted here that while medieval moralists from time to time had assigned a specific animal to a sin and while others upon occasion had treated sin as a disease, it was Spenser's particular genius to combine these ancillary motifs, as if to lathe poor Avarice and its fellows with more and more images of disgust. In this and similar matters, Carol V. Kaske furnishes an insightful discussion of

Spenser's place in the theological aesthetic of his times in her volume *Spenser and Biblical Poetics* (Ithaca: Cornell University Press, 1999).

21. Although there's not space to look at everything in so brief a treatise as this one, we should at least note here that traditional allegory—that is, the story of a human being as a human being touring about to meet the sins in a metaphorical landscape—was also very much in play during this same period of the physical imagination and gave us, again most famously from today's point of view, images ranging from ones like those of Dante to those of John Bunyan; and from an earlier point of view, images like those in *The Shepherd of Hermas*, Hermas being the author and accounted as one of the Apostolic Fathers, though little is actually known of him. *The Shepherd* tells the tale of a series of visions, in the third of which Hermas is shown a tower, i.e., the church, which is being built with many stones, all of which fit neatly together. Rejected and to the side of the building site, however, are piles of round white stones that, his lady-guide informs him, are the wealthy. When tribulation comes, she says, they always deny their Lord because of their wealth and the press of their business affairs. As a result, they can be of no use until their wealth is hewn, quite literally, from them (*Vision 3*, 20:1–20:11).

The telling point here, however, is what the lady condemns. It is the apostasy to which the wealth and greed of the faithful have led them and not the wealth itself that is the impediment. Moreover, poverty per se is neither a requirement nor a *summum bonum* in the allegory. Rather, self-sufficiency is treated as being desirable because it can not only foil avarice but also give one enough with which to relieve the poor.

Like the *Psychomachia* that worked by personification, the *Hermas,* which worked by human example, is the birthing cry of a form of Christian moral instruction *cum* entertainment that will give Western art its other, closely akin, principal source of inspiration. Certainly, in literature, Dante, Langland, Chaucer, and Bunyan all do come to us by way of it. So close is the affiliation in Dante, for instance, that one does not need a critic's skills to perceive in Hermas's guide a kind of prototype of Dante's Virgil in her function and of his Beatrice in her perfection.

22. All of Prudentius's personifications are female, a point that has caused—and should cause!—considerable scholarly concern. An excellent overview of both the literature and the psycho-theological implications may be found in Nugent's essay, and I urge the reader to pursue this influential and still vital part of Prudentius's legacy there.

23. Lines 407–32

24. Lines 449–54

25. Lines 464–66

26. Lines 467–69

27. Lines 494b–96

28. While much of the paraphrase used here is my own, the quoted material is as translated on http://www.rich mond.edu/~wstevens/grvaltexts/psychomachia.html. Interested readers may want to look there for a complete, though prose-rendered, translation. Those who wish to see a copy

of the Latin text and of the material in its original poetic format will find a very useful presentation of it at http://ccat.sas.upenn.edu/jod/texts/psychomachia/psychomachia.html.

29. Lines 497–504

30. The concept presented here is, in its mention of inventiveness, consonant with that of Evagrios of Pontus (346–99 C.E.). A desert father and contemporary of Saint Augustine probably as well as of Prudentius, he went in 382 from Egypt to Asia Minor to establish a rule of desert asceticism there and wrote his *Praktikos* as a rule for his monks. (Evagrios is best known, by the way, as the abbot who taught that women and bishops were the greatest temptations to monks and that both should always be engaged only as such.) In *Praktikos*, Evagrios employs the same notion as John Cassian about there being an octad of sins, which he lists as the customary seven deadly sins plus impurity. It is in his discussion of greed itself, however, that Evagrios is not only most interesting to us, but also most specific about the sin's singular dependence on the "what if's" and the "it might be's" of life and about its proclivity for wanting to create provision for that which is not yet even real.

"Evagrios, however, sheds some interesting light on the subject [i.e., greed] by examining not the sin's most superficial and obvious forms, but what in the contemplative life were its insidious temptations: 'Avarice suggests to the mind a lengthy old age, inability to perform manual labor (at some future date), famines that are sure to come, sickness that will visit us, the pinch of poverty, the great shame that comes

Figure 1. Michel Bohbot. *The Greenspan Buddha.* © 2000. All rights reserved.

Figure 2. Pieter Breugel the Elder. *Big Fish Eat Little Fish*, Inv. 7875. Albertina, Wien.

Figure 3. Hieronymus Bosch. *Avarice, from the Seven Deadly Sins series.* Scala / Art Resource, NY. Museo del Prado, Madrid.

Figure 4. Hieronymus Bosch. *The Haywain.* Triptych, ca. 1485–1490. Erich Lessing / Art Resource, NY. Museo del Prado, Madrid.

Figure 5. James Ensor. *The Seven Deadly Sins.* © 2003 Artists Rights Society (ARS), New York / SABAM, Brussels. Wake Forest University Print Collection. Photo: Martine Sherril.

Figure 6. Otto Dix. *Sieben Todsünden,* 1933 (Karton). © VG-bild-Kunst, Bonn.
Galerie der Stadt, Stuttgart.

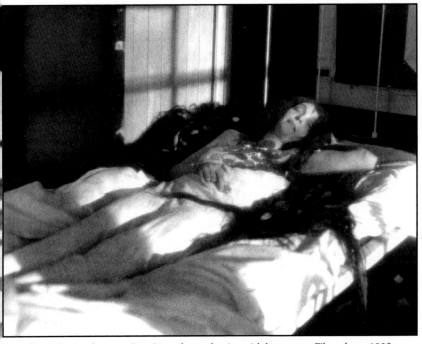

Figure 7. *Greed.* Actress Zasu Pitts, shown sleeping with her money. Film release: 1925.
Courtesy of the Everett Collection.

Figure 8. *Wall Street.* Actor Michael Douglas. Film release: 1987.

from accepting the necessities of life from others.'

"Evagrios goes right to the heart of the matter: avarice is not defined by pure material greed, but by the principle of *thinking about what does not yet exist* [emphasis his], a kind of preoccupation with imaginary or future things such as hopes and fears. That one could be greedy about what one fears is a subtlety that escapes our ordinary thinking. The distinctive feature here is that the future enters into the sin. This differentiates it from *sadness (tristitia,* often related to envy and sloth), in which the future is replaced by the past and present, and which has to do with more immediate deprivations." Paul Jordan-Smith, "Seven (and More) Deadly Sins," 41–42.

31. Lines 551b–569a

32. Paul himself furnishes the foundation for this association in Col. 3:5 when he speaks of "greed, which is idolatry."

33. One of the more intriguing imagistic "threads" here is that of the bestiaries that became enormously popular during the eleventh through the fifteenth centuries in Europe. Because they have not survived as a vital art form into our time, there's little justification for including a sustained mention of them in the body of this paper. It is appropriate, however, before we entirely close our overview of the physical imagination to at least mention them as a variant on allegorical treatment of greed and the other vices (though they dealt with animal character as examples of the sins rather than as personifications per se) and to note that the subgenre had its origins in another early work, *Physiologus,* which was translated from its original, second-century Greek into Latin

sometime before 388, or during Prudentius's lifetime.

We should note as well that in the visual arts, especially in the iconography of a faith with what was increasingly an essentially illiterate laity, the image of the tree became the dominant allegorical one. So familiar was this depiction that Chaucer's Parson, for example, begins his torturous disquisition on the seven deadlies with tree imagery. A perversion of a sort of the Tree of Life theme, the metaphorical presentation of sin as a trunk, the seven deadlies as its branches, and human woes as its fruit became a pictorial Tree of Death.

There were variations, of course, on this basic arrangement, but the central motif held, as did not only the popularity of images but also their official usage. The *Patrologia Latina* asserts the worth of images for teaching "untutored men" to regulate their conduct in accord with Christian ways. This stance, like so much else in medieval and Renaissance Christianity, has its roots in Gregory the Great, who urged iconography and allegorical painting upon the church so that "those who know no letters may yet read."

Medieval British churches, in particular, abound with the tree images: Crostwight, Saint Edmundsburg and Ipswich, Hessett, South Leigh, etc. An excellent website, http://www.paintedchurch.org provides an armchair tour of these and many more frescoes. Readers may also find more about the *Patrologia Latina* at the same site.

34. Paradoxically, it was in the greed of the Darwinian worldview of the survival of the fittest that Western intellectuals found temporary surcease. For a very cogent, if less dispas-

sionate presentation of this position, the reader may wish to see Cornelius G. Hunter, *Darwin's God: Evolution and the Problem of Evil* (Grand Rapids: Brazos Books, 2001), 10 and following. Darwin was "motivated toward evolution not by direct evidence in favor of his new theory, but by problems with the common notion of divine creation" that could not resolve the conundrum of a benevolent God as source and ruler of a malevolent existence.

The same general thesis also informs *Charles Darwin— The Power of Place: Volume II of a Biography* (New York: Alfred A. Knopf, 2002) by Janet Browne, who incorporates in the broader scope of her study, as a leitmotif, the nineteenth century's need to lionize Darwin and his theory even in the face of serious questions about the theory itself.

Locating the source of greed and all her kith and kin in biology rather than theology may have been a solution to the problems of justifying the ways of God to man by a remove of only one, but it at least had the advantage of some immediate solace. The rub lay, of course, in the fact that surcease is rarely permanent; it certainly was not in this case, for the twentieth century had yet to play its hand. What Professor Solomon Schimmel of Hebrew College calls "amoral psychology" and deplores as "secular psychology" was to proffer yet another, though hardly unrelated, pathogenesis for greed and all her kin.

35. One of the happier results of the recent currency of sin among us and of our interest in it occurred when, as a major component of its Fall 2001 season, the Metropolitan Museum of Art chose to show the prints and drawings of

Pieter Bruegel the Elder. Of those works, one of the four the *New York Times* reproduced and emphasized in its coverage was *Big Fish Eat Little Fish*. It was, to say the least, an example of exquisitely prescient timing.

36. This kind of broad statement seeks to speak the truth, of course, in its overall effect more than in its particulars. In this instance, for example, it is absolutely true that while Karl Marx was developing and refining his theories of the town square and the dialectical materialism that would lead the Western world into total upheaval only fifty years later—the first volume of *Das Kapital* was published in 1867—Wagner was composing and taking into production *Der Ring des Nibelungen* (1853–1874). It is incontestably true as well that there never could be a more Olympian treatment of greed than Wagner's. The point, however, is that though both men would exert enormous influence over their own and subsequent times, Wagner's would remain primarily in the field of music while Marx's would be specific to the study of greed and all her applications.

37. It was the facile and constantly reflective Pope who also observed of his time that: "Satan now is wiser than of yore, / And tempts by making rich, not making poor." *Moral Essays* 1.35, I.

38. Admittedly, other than being opposed to both of them, Christianity, from its earliest writings, has never been uniformly certain about its own thinking with regard to the nature of evil or of sin. Where Saint Paul presents sin as a violation of the natural law and presents it as universally present (Rom. 2:14–16), the burden of the epistle of Saint

James is that sin has its origins in the human will and the responsibility of the individual. Much of the Johannine canon presents sin as consisting essentially in disbelief in Jesus as Messiah. Manichaeism, a large and influential sect within patristic Christianity that finally was condemned as heresy, taught that evil was a substance and creation inherently evil. Saint Augustine was himself a Manichaeian for nine years; and it is in part his own struggle with that doctrine that leads finally to the *Confessions* and to Augustine's very influential doctrine of the divine necessity of free will in the creature as the origin of sin.

39. Schimmel, 5.
40. This kind of sanguine application of religious teaching even to a secular world is particularly evident in Jewish thinking. Thus in the imaging of Judaism, forebear of Christianity but culturally distinct from it, the *yetzer hara,* or evil impulse, is indeed guided by Satan. It is held in balance, however, by the *yetzer hatov,* or good impulse, which drives humanity toward the worthy and creative use of all things. Absent a Reformation and the spiritual costs of political ascendency, such vivid imagery has managed to sustain effectually the vivid precepts of Maimonides, the great twelfth-century rabbi, who taught that one who would live rightly must, within each moment, live as if his or her next action would set the whole world atilt, spinning toward either the benevolent *yetzer hatov* or, most frightening of all, toward the greedy *yetzer hara.*
41. Schimmel, 10.
42. Our own times have put an interesting, additional twist on

this. In a sinewy essay, "There's Something Wrong with Evil," for her weekly "The Close Reader" feature of 6 October 2002 (39), *New York Times Book Review* commentator Judith Shulevitz observed, "Philosophers have spent the past 300 years trying to come up with a better definition of evil than the one religion seems to offer, or so one philosopher, Susan Neiman, says in a new book, *Evil in Modern Thought: An Alternative History of Philosophy* (Princeton: Princeton University Press). This may seem perfectly obvious, but as a philosophical claim it is fairly controversial, because most historians of the subject would say that modern philosophy has been so anxious to differentiate itself from theology that it refused to talk about evil at all."

Picking up the question current in some conversations about whether or not the religiously motivated violence of a zealot like Osama Bin Laden is to be forgiven or at the very least evaluated as a result not of evil but of false belief, Shulevitz comes down sharply on the side of no forgiveness, noting as she does so that, "The idea that we judge evil men by their actions, not by the content or intensity of their beliefs, may be postmodern in the sense that it succeeds the modern Enlightenment definition of evil, but it does not lead to moral relativism. On the contrary, it leads to its opposite—moral absolutism—since it presumes a universal standard by which to judge behavior." Shulevitz concludes that in such times as ours, the Bin Ladens and the suicide bombers of this world are more terrifying than ever before because "they force us to face the chilly reality of a world in which sincerity and morality have nothing to do with each other."

43. Just as *Big Fish* was to become a visual proof text of a shift
    in the common imagination of Western Christian culture,
    so too Milton's *Paradise Lost,* coming a century later, was to
    serve as a kind of highly imagistic verbal one. Perhaps more
    even than a proof text, though, Milton's work actually
    functioned as a bridge between the two worlds of physical
    and intellectual imagining; for while his *Paradise* retains
    much of the imagery, color, personification, and divine glory
    of earlier times and of the poet's own deep faith, it, in its
    purposes, admits to the general conversation a central theme
    that dominates the centuries between him and us. What
    Milton set out with faith and optimism to do was justify the
    ways of a God in whom he believed to a humanity that he
    regarded as being of incomplete and transient understand-
    ing. By arguing that humanity fails to perceive the rightness
    of the world because we cannot apprehend the purposes of
    God, Milton, however unintentionally, legitimated the
    question; and by doing that, he introduced the agonies and
    the glories of theodicy to a restive, knowledge-enamored
    new society. (The anachronism here almost establishes the
    impact of Milton's work more succinctly than could any-
    thing else. *Theodicy* was first coined forty years after Milton
    in 1710 by Leibnitz in his *Essais de Théodicée sur la bonte de
    Dieu.*)

44. Although Silas Marner and Scrooge stand as early moder-
    nity's best-known literary images of greed in human and/or
    subjective form, in the same period Feodor Dostoyevsky, that
    great giant of Russian literature, produced an equally power-
    ful and long-lived image of greed, albeit by means of an

onion. Dostoyevsky, in his *The Brothers Karamazov*, relates the parable of a miserly old widow who was in hell for her avariciousness. Her guardian angel, seeing the poor soul in such agony, petitioned God for mercy, using as the justification for her release the fact that once upon a time she had given an onion to a poor woman in need. God agreed to her release if the angel would agree to take an onion and hold it above the fires of hell in such a way as to allow the widow to grasp it and thereby pull herself free. The angel accepted God's terms and did as instructed, the widow successfully grasped the onion, and all was about to be resolved happily. The difficulty God had foreseen arose, however, when all the other souls in hell observed a rescue in progress. They immediately rushed to grab and claw at the widow in attempts to ride her and her onion into freedom for themselves. Because souls weigh very little, the onion held all this additional burden without compromise right up until the widow, greedy to the end, began to kick and beat her fellow-damned off her onion. As she swung and shoved and flailed, the onion first began to pop and then finally broke beneath her thrashing; and the old widow dropped forever back into hell to spend eternity with those to whom she had, in her greed, denied a share in her near-release.

Probably in early modern Western literature, the other most memorable image of greed's horrors by association with an object rather than with characters per se is D. H. Lawrence's story "The Rocking Horse Winner." Here Paul, the young son of a disastrously overextended family, discovers that by some unknown means he can see and articulate the names of winning race horses, but only if and when he rides his own rocking horse at an exhaustive rate of ferocity. The story, predictably, shows Paul's greedy relatives driving the boy to rock faster and faster, harder and harder, until he at last dies before their very eyes of his exertions. The poignancy of a rocking horse as the most beloved and familiar toy in early modern childhood lends Lawrence's use of it a peculiar and compelling potency.

45. While Nietzsche's is a colorful projection of what was to happen, his is not the only, or even a complete, explanation. When greed rises to primacy of place in the human conversation, historically one or another of two configurations is always prior and operative. The first is itself twofold, namely: greed always "flourishes in a social environment abounding with wealth" (Schimmel, 262, n1); and second, where wealth flourishes, greed will always find those who will praise her and before whom she can preen. The other, stranger, more potent configuration is that human fascination with greed burgeons in periods of end-times thinking. When these two things occur in conjunction with one another—when, that is, a period of expanding wealth and an era of heightened end-times anxiety coincide—greed as a result becomes exponentially both more present and more commented upon. Obviously the confluence of "abounding" wealth and apocalyptic anxieties has informed the decades since Nietzsche and must be held partially responsible for our present illness of "infectious greed."

It is of some interest or amusement perhaps to note that the first, serious Christian exploration of the connection between greed and eschatology was also one primarily of cause and effect and comes out of the patristic period. Lactantius, a rhetorician and the tutor of the Emperor Constantine's son, lived during the third century in what was still a very polytheistic culture. From the perspective of the centuries, he would probably be regarded now as having been as much an apologist for monotheism as for Christianity, in fact. Lactantius made his case for that position on the basis that before there were the many gods of Greco-Roman culture, there had been a pre-times of monotheism, a kind of Golden Age or string of them, in which, out of fear of God and concern for the community, there was no greed or, as he called it, cupidity. All things depended from God and were God's and were to be accounted for to God. But when Lactantius's *aurea tempora* were lost, they were not lost to cataclysm. Rather, they were eroded away. They were lost to a slow, deadly slide into a polytheism that came of worshiping the immediate functions of God in order to the better manipulate them to one's own advantage. Thus, Lactantius argues, it was greed that made humanity's expulsion from the golden ages inevitable. Greed and her offspring pride or, as Lactantius saw it, the unfettered individualism that was born of them, were therefore both the prophets and the cause of cataclysm. (Much of this story as well as the interpretation of its implications I owe to Professor Richard Newhauser. The matter of interpretation informs in particular his "Avarice and the Apocalypse," in *The Christian Use of the Golden Age Myth*, ed. R. Landes and D. Van Meters [Oxford: Oxford University Press, forthcoming]. For a more sustained presentation of Lactantius's story itself, the reader should see Newhauser, *The Early History of Greed: The Sin of Avarice in Early Medieval Thought and Literature* [Cambridge: Cambridge University Press, 2000], 18–21.)

In writing his more or less mythical history of our genesis, Lactantius managed to establish—or perhaps just remark—what still appertains today as the immutable, if largely subliminal, bond in Christian thinking between end-times and greed in terms both of their simultaneity and the causative effect of the latter upon the former. The fact that Lactantius may seem more quaint than informative to us does not necessarily mean, in other words, that he was in error in his premise, just in his proofs.

It certainly would be more than sanguine of us to conclude that apocalyptic fears simply create a nurturing hotbed of growth for greed in and of themselves. So long as both Christian thought and cultural theology, however— and thanks in part, no doubt, to Lactantius—hold that the end of time is coming because of rampant greed and/or that the time just before apocalypse is to be characterized by rampant greed, good Christian folk will always find more of it in periods of heightened eschatological worry, because that is when the Christianized are most conditioned to go looking for it.

It is also true that end-times anxiety in and of itself creates a generalized and brooding sense of culpability. With the brief exception of the just-concluded 400 years of militant Protestantism and Euro-American expansion, we human beings have known, without having to be told, that what we have, we have either to the disadvantage of, or at the expense of, another; and we have known as well that there is no mortal help for us in that, either here or in the darkness ahead. In such a psychological climate, the very starkness of no tomorrow inevitably serves as a blank and well-lit backdrop where greed can find no shadow in which to hide.

Just here, I would be unfaithful to my own industry if I did not cite one further and very contemporary example of the dynamic that accrues from the simultaneity of eschatology, wealth, an increase in greed, and an increase in popular obsession with greed. One of the more engaging things for me about the book industry is the way in which it consistently is both reactive and proactive within its culture at one and the same time. That is, book making both reflects and helps to cause the currents in our lives.

In 2001, for the first time since such records began to be kept, the best-selling book in America in both the fiction and the nonfiction categories was a religion book, both of them published by a religion house. The *Left Behind* series of novels, which is published by Tyndale House and that when last I checked was well beyond the 40 million mark in the units sold of it and its related products, is pure apocalypticism. It is, from beginning to end, a fictive presentation of what the end of the world will be like according to the teachings of what Christians called predispensational millennarian theology, a theology whose horrific conceits—the mark of the Beast, 666, the fiery lake, the rapture—are probably, I would suggest, the dominant ones as well in American folk culture.

Left Behind's counterpart in the top nonfiction slot was *The Prayer of Jabez*, published by Multnomah Press, and now so successful as to have spawned a whole industry of Jabez products. Called by Brian Britt, professor and head of the Religious Studies Program at Virginia Tech, "a remarkably Nietzschean take on Christianity," the prayer of the book's title is a petition to God to expand one's borders, such a prayer being empowered by the nineteenth-century premise that God wants the faithful all to be prosperous ("Nietzsche and *The Prayer of Jabez*," *Sightings*, 9 August 2002. The Martin Marty Center at the University of Chicago Divinity School). The fact that others may be inconvenienced or even compromised by this aggrandizement of some of us should not be a concern of any real significance, because one of the by-products of the prayers' success will be an increase in their sphere of Christian influence and in what they have to share.

My point here is that regardless of what you or I may think of such books or the validity of their theses does not matter nearly so much as does the fact that millions of my fellow Christians and millions of our fellow Americans do hold them to be, if not true, then pleasurable to contemplate. In effect, the nation's cash registers in 2001 confirmed the complementary coexistence of end-times fascination and preoccupation with greed more irrefutably than any of us ever could have.

46. It is probably worth noting here that while, academically speaking, the space between Adam Smith's "Invisible Hand"

and Marx's dialectical materialism is little more than one of decreasingly imagistic conversation and increasingly cerebral articulation, concomitant with that slide has been a century and a half of unprecedented war, bloodshed, social unrest, and human agony.

In fairness, one should also acknowledge that Smith was a deeply religious man. In attributing the mystery of the ongoing nature of human affairs to the machinations of an invisible and divine hand, however, he produced one of Western history's more prominent, lasting, and deftly secularized images about the mechanisms of greed. It is in fact ironic that this image, which the father of classical economics refined and promulgated in his 1776 masterpiece, *An Inquiry into the Nature and Causes of the Wealth of Nations*, enjoys a present currency he could never have foreseen; its processes and their study are now part of Game Theory mathematics, or the science of rewards and strategies.

47.   In exemplifying the "visual arts" only in terms of painting and cinema, I act with apologies to those whose art form, while technically performing, is nonetheless quite definitely visual as well. Dance in particular has made a considerable contribution to the cultural coversation about greed over the past century. Most remarked upon perhaps is the 1933 production of the *Seven Deadly Sins* by George Balanchine, Bertolt Brecht, and Kurt Weill. Somewhat less famously, Pina Bausch also used Weill's score to choreograph another production of the sins; but the most current engagement of note was the presentation of the *Seven Deadly Sins* on the stage of the Ted Shawn Theater at the Jacob's Pillow Dance

Festival in July 2002. Seven different choreographers created pieces for the production that was remarkable, among other things, for the sheer quality and stature of the dancers whom it attracted to perform. Annie-B Parsons of Big Dance Theater danced "Greed," though in keeping with Roman Catholic theology since Aquinas, "Pride," danced by Robert La Fosse, served as the finale.

48. This latter concept of greed as the hallmark of the oppressor, while it has its clear beginnings in Marx and his fellow nineteenth-century intellectuals, was promulgated during the nineteenth and early twentieth centuries not only in revolutionary nonfiction but also in wildly popular books like Frank Norris's *McTeague: A Story of San Francisco* (see essay) and Sinclair Lewis's *The Jungle,* a shift toward the political uses of entertainment that has had, and continues to have, a significant impact on the publishing business.

49. Gekko's stance of praising greed to audiences who already love it and are profiting from it fits a pattern that has not been suggested in the body of this essay but is worthy of passing mention here, namely that odes to greed are not a peculiarly twentieth-century phenomenon. Generally speaking, in Western culture, times of high and general affluence have always evoked such paeans. For instance, Rome's great orator, Cicero, in his *De officiis,* taught that the desire to increase one's goods is a legitimate and valuable human endeavor and that *avaritia* is nothing more than the misuse of a laudable trait. In more recent time, Adam Smith's quip that it is not from the goodness of the baker's heart that we obtain our bread is almost a staple of folk wisdom more

than 200 years after he said it.

Perhaps the two clearest examples of the phenomenon, however—the two most analogous to the impact of Gekko's words—come from fifteenth-century Italy and eighteenth-century England. Thus, in the first half of the fifteenth century, in the midst of a thriving and expanding Europe, Poggio Bracciolini's dialogue *On Avarice* defends greed as being natural, useful, and necessary because it teaches us to provide for ourselves and avoid inconveniences. (Take note the pronoun of choice here; for what we also find in Bracciolini's widely circulated apologia is an early still-frame of the late-Renaissance shift from what would once have been greed, the sin, to a nuanced and precapitalism/capitalism-enabling notion of acquisition and acquisitiveness as not necessarily sinful.)

Two hundred years later, Bernard Mandeville (1670–1733), a physician, wrote *The Fable of the Bees* praising greed for an increasingly affluent Britain. In effect, *The Fable* did for greed what Voltaire and *Candide* did for Christian optimism and, indirectly, for blasphemy. Kant in particular admired Mandeville's apologia, and *The Fable* can defensibly be regarded as a precursor to utilitarianism. Interested readers will most assuredly want to look up John Portmann's recent *In Defense of Sin* (New York: Palgrave/St. Martin's Press, 2001) for an especially delightful modernization of Mandeville's "The Grumbling Hive: or, Knaves Turned Honest" from *Bees*.

50. In all fairness to ourselves and in the name of containing hyperbole, I should add as well that near the end of the

twentieth century we began to see, in the visual arts anyway, a shift away from regarding greed as a mark of the oppressor and as a characteristic of someone other than ourselves. One thinks, for example, of works like those of the sculptor Mark Quinn or the Los Manos artists in Chicago or even of Brad Pitt and Morgan Freeman in *Seven* where the denial of such deflection is integral to the narrative.

51. I am indebted for these images and data to J. Bradford DeLong, professor of economics at the University of California, Berkeley, who in a Carnegie-sponsored essay titled "Robber Barons" comments as well, with some bemusement, about the causative agencies and conditions underlying times of such disproportionate accumulations of personal wealth. Whether the reader adheres to a Lactantian-like, apocalyptic correlation for explanation or joins DeLong in regarding such issues as the "big questions" still to be resolved, he or she could find few pieces more illuminating than "Robber Barons," a full text of which may be found most easily at http://econ161.berkeley.edu/Econ_Articles/carnegie/delong_moscow_paper2.html.

52. As is so frequently true when speaking of greed in any of her presentations, there is a kind of pleasurable easiness in pointing one's finger at another and crying, "Guiltier than I," as if to exercise some kind of self-absolution thereby. The truth, as I have already said, is that anyone who empowers the greedy out of his or her own self-interest is likewise greedy.

Thus, the accusations of simony as a fatal flaw of the ordained have become such easy, albeit partial, explanations for the Reformation as to have become little more than convenient cliches. Historical records cast a wider net, however. The greed of the laity in controlling shrines and reliquaries and healing sites operated as a sort of lay simony, becoming eventually as corrupt and corrupting as the business of buying and selling salvation. For a particularly engrossing overview of this late medieval phenomenon, the reader will want to read Craig Harline's *Miracles at the Jesus Oak* (New York: Doubleday, 2003), especially as it treats of the nefariousness of the Tailors' Guild in Ghent.

53. As is true with the work of many major artists, the Ars Media website is an excellent and accessible source for both viewing Donizetti's canvases and reading some of his aesthetic and philosophic commentary. *Avarizia* herself may be located at: http://www.arsmedia.net/donizetti-visicapital/avarizia.htm.

54. So as not to mislead, I should note here that avarice's was not the panel painted first. Donizetti completed envy, a horizontal study, in 1995, showing it first and alone. Pride, a vertical, came later that year. In accordance with the teaching of Roman Catholic theology since Aquinas that Pride is the prince of the sins, pride's panel is now shown just to avarice's right.

55. Isaiah 45:7 (*KJV*).

Bibliography

Bazen, Ken. *The Seven Perennial Sins and Their Offspring*. New York: Continuum, 2002.

Bernstein, Peter L. *The Power of Gold*. New York: Wiley, 2000.

Browne, Janet. *Charles Darwin—The Power of Place: Volume II of a Biography*. New York: Alfred A. Knopf, 2002.

Chesterton, Gilbert K. *St. Thomas Aquinas*. New York: Image Books, 2001.
——— *Orthodoxy*. New York: Image Books, 1990.

Crossan, John Dominic. *Excavating Jesus*. San Francisco: HarperSanFrancisco, 2001.

Cruver, Brian. *The Anatomy of Greed*. New York: Carroll & Graf Publishers, 2002.

Davis, David Brion. *In the Image of God: Religion, Moral Values, and Our Heritage of Slavery*. New Haven: Yale University Press, 2001.

DeLong, J. Bradford. "Robber Barons." http://econ161.berkeley.edu/Econ_Articles/carnegie/delong_moscow_paper2.html. Accessed 1 November 2002.

Dorff, Elliot N. *To Do Right and Good: A Jewish Approach to Modern Social Ethics*. Philadelphia: Jewish Lights, 2002.

Dunnam, Maxie, and Kimberly Dunnam Reisman, *The Workbook on the Seven Deadly Sins*. Nashville: Upper Room, 1997.

"Evil." *Parabola*, vol. 24, no. 4 (1999).

Fairlie, Henry. *The Seven Deadly Sins*. Notre Dame: University of Notre Dame Press, 1995.

Fox, Matthew. *Sins of the Spirit, Blessings of the Flesh*. New York: Harmony Books, 1999.

Freedman, David Noel. *The Nine Commandments*. New York: Doubleday, 2000.

Hourihane, Colum, ed. *Virtue and Vice: The Personifications in the Index of Christian Art*. Princeton: Princeton University Press, 2000.

Hunter, Cornelius G. *Darwin's God: Evolution and the Problem of Evil*. Grand Rapids: Brazos Books, 2001.

Jennings, Kate. *Moral Hazards*. New York: Fourth Estate, 2002.

Jordan-Smith, Paul. "Seven (and More) Deadly Sins." *Parabola*, vol. 10, no. 4 (1985): 34–45.

Kaske, Carol V. *Spenser and Biblical Poetics*. Ithaca: Cornell University Press, 1999.

Kisly, Lorraine, ed. *Watch and Pray: Christian Teachings on the Practice of Prayer*. New York: Bell Tower, 2002.

Knitter, Paul F., and Chandra Muzaffar, eds. *Subverting Greed: Religious Perspectives in the Global Economy*. Maryknoll: Orbis Books, 2002.

Kishk, Sheikh 'Abd al-Hamid. *Dealing with Lust and Greed According to Islam*. London: Dar Al Taqawa, Ltd., 1995.

Lukacs, John. *At the End of an Age*. New Haven: Yale University Press, 2002.

Martin Marty Center at the University of Chicago Divinity School. "Nietzsche and *The Prayer of Jabez*." *Sightings*, 9 August 2002.

Mikva, Rachel. *Broken Tablets: Restoring the Ten Commandments and Ourselves*. Philadelphia: Jewish Lights, 1999.

Neiman, Susan, *Evil in Modern Thought: An Alternative History of Philosophy*. Princeton: Princeton University Press, 2002.

Nelson-Pallmeyer, Jack. *School of Assassins: Guns, Greed, and Globalization*. Maryknoll: Orbis Books, 2001.

Newhauser, Richard "Avarice and the Apocalypse." In *The Christian Use of the Golden Age Myth,* ed. R. Landes and D. Van Meters. Oxford: Oxford University Press, forthcoming.

———. *The Early History of Greed: The Sin of Avarice in Early Medieval Thought and Literature*. Cambridge: Cambridge University Press, 2000.

Nugent, S. Georgia. "Virtus or Virago? The Female Personifications of Prudentius's *Psychomachia.*" In *Virtue and Vice: The Personifications in the Index of Christian Art,* ed. Colum Hourihan. Princeton: Princeton University Press, 2000.

Portmann, John. *In Defense of Sin.* New York: Palgrave/St. Martin's Press, 2001.

Prudentius, Aurelius Clemens. *Psychomachia.* http://www.richmond.edu/~wstevens/grvaltexts/psychomachia.html; http://ccat.sas.upenn.edu/jod/texts/psychomachia/psychomachia.html. Accessed 1 November 2002.

Rabinowitz, Dr. Robert. "The SEC as Spiritual Apparatus" *e-CLAL* (July 2002). http://www.beliefnet.com/story/109/story_10913.html. Accessed 1 November 2002.

Reed, Gerard. *C. S. Lewis Explores Vice and Virtue.* Kansas City: Beacon Hill, 2001.

Schimmel, Solomon. *The Seven Deadly Sins: Jewish, Christian, and Classical Reflections on Human Psychology.* New York: Oxford University Press, 1997.

Shulevitz, Judith. "There's Something Wrong with Evil" (review of Susan Neiman, *Evil in Modern Thought: An Alternative History of Philosophy*). *New York Times Book Review,* 6 October 2002, 39.

Simon, Katherine G. *Moral Questions in the Classroom.* New Haven: Yale University Press, 2001.

Stalker, James. *The Seven Deadly Sins and the Seven Cardinal Virtues.* Colorado Springs: NavPress, 1998.

Watson, Lyall. *Dark Nature: A Natural History of Evil.* New York: HarperCollins, 1995.

Index

Britt, Brian, 79
Brothers Karamazov (Dostoyevsky), 73–74n44
Brown, Janet, 68–69n34
Bruegel, Pieter, the Elder, 30–32, 38, 41, 69–70n35
Buddhism, 5, 10, 11, 13–14
Bunyan, John, 64n21

cable of meaning, religion as, 1–6
Candide (Voltaire), 82n45
capitalism, 33
Cassian, John, xi, 55–56n8, 66n30
Charles Darwin—The Power of Place (Browne), 68–69n34
Chaucer, Geoffrey, 45, 68n33
Christian church, 23, 61–62n15; fathers of, 58n12; women and homosexuals in, 5
Christianity, 9, 21, 25, 37, 55–56n8; eschatology, 75–79n45; ideal of, 22; nature of evil and, 70–71n38; opening decades of, 59–60n15; Renaissance, 68n33; scripture of, 57n10; theology of, 54n6;

vice and sin and, 12. *See also* Reformation *and specific Christian philosophers and theologians*
Christian Use of the Golden Age Myth, The (Landes and Van Meters, eds.), 76–77
Christmas Carol, A (Dickens), 39
Cicero, 81n49
Clemens, Aurelius, 24
"Close Reader, The" (Schulevitz), 72n42
communism, 34. *See also* Marx, Karl
compassion, 36
Confessions (Augustine), 71n38
corporeality, 1, 5–6, 33. *See also* physical imagination
covetousness, 13, 57–58n11. *See also* avarice; cupidity
Crossan, John Dominic, 61n15
culture, 3, 4, 10; praise of greed in, 81–82n49
Cupiditas (Boniface), 62–63
cupidity, 58n12, 76n45. *See also* avarice; covetousness

dance, 80–81n47
Dante, 47–48, 64–65n21
Dark Nature (Watson), 8
Darwin, Charles, 31, 68–69n34

"There's Something Wrong with Evil" (Shulevitz), 71–72n42
Thrift *(Psychomachia)*, 28, 38
tree image, 68n33

United States, 4, 44. *See also* America
U.S. Senate Banking Committee, 59n13
Utilitarianism, 82n49

values, system of. *See* morality
Vatican II, 5
vice, 10, 12; sin and, 57n9; spiritualization of, 54n6. *See also* sin
victimization, 35
virtue, theology of, 10
Visuddhimagga, 14
Voltaire, 82n49

Wagner, Richard, 70n36
Wall Street (film), 43
Watson, Lyall, 8
wealth, 21, 43–44, 75n45, 78n
Wealth of Nations, The (Smith), 79–80n46
Weill, Kurt, 80n47
Welch, Jack, 44
western thought, 37–38, 40
Wittenberg, 32, 33, 46. *See also* Luther, Martin; Reformation
women, 5
World Trade Towers, 45
World War II, 4

yetzer hara (evil impulse), 55n7, 71n40
yetzer hatov (good impulse), 71n40